MW00529045

JUDSON PRESS
PUBLISHERS SINCE 1824

Distinctly Baptist

Proclaiming Identity in a New Generation

BRIAN C. BREWER, EDITOR

Foreword by David W. Bebbington

JUDSON PRESS

PUBLISHERS SINCE 1824

VALLEY FORGE, PA

Interior design by Beth Oberholtzer.

Cover design by Tobias Becker and Bird Box Graphic Design, www.birdboxdesign.com.

Library of Congress Cataloging-in-Publication data

Distinctly Baptist : proclaiming identity in a new generation / Brian C. Brewer, editor ; foreword by David W. Bebbington. — 1st ed.
    p. cm.
    ISBN 978-0-8170-1698-2 (pbk. : alk. paper) 1. Baptists—Doctrines. 2. Baptists—Sermons. 3. Sermons, American—21st century. 4. Baptist theological seminaries—Sermons. I. Brewer, Brian C.
    BX6331.3.D57 2011
    230'.6—dc23
                                2011017117

Printed in the U.S.A.
First Edition, 2011.

friends of
JUDSON PRESS
PUBLISHERS SINCE 1824

Contents

Foreword

Three of the important trends of thought in the contemporary world relate to community, authority, and the visual. There has been, in the first place, a growth in appreciation of human solidarity, encompassing both a rising sense of the value of corporate life and a corresponding decline in unquestioning praise for individualism. One symptom has been increasing respect for the high valuation of social groups in the third world; another has been the emergence of the political theory labeled 'communitarianism.' Secondly, there has been a questioning of authority in the name of freedom. Traditional ways have been challenged and earlier social roles have been transformed. The most striking instances have probably been the feminist uprising against patriarchy and the demand for an end to discrimination on grounds of race. The third tendency has been the inexorable advance of the visual at the expense of the verbal. Television is the preferred medium of the many; radio is for the few. The movie rather than the novel is the standard point of cultural reference. What is seen is what leaves its mark. There have, of course, been many other developments such as the growth of prosperity in the post-war world and the information revolution of the computer age, but the three phenomena relating to community, authority, and the visual have become some of the most salient phenomena of the day.

To these trends Baptists can speak with peculiar persuasiveness. They believe in a community, the gathered church. The centrality of their churchmanship has sometimes been obscured by an ill-judged attempt to justify their principles in terms of individualism. But Baptists assert the obligation of Christians to form committed communities of like-minded people. Again, they believe in sharing authority.

While recognizing the need for wise leadership of the church, they insist that every church member has a duty to choose the leaders and to hold them to account. While acknowledging, too, the supreme earthly authority of biblical revelation, they regard it as essential for every church member to have the privilege of discerning how the Bible applies to church life in our day. And they believe in the power of the visual. The ceremony from which they take their name is a visible sign of the totality of Christian commitment. Baptists do not neglect the outward display of inward conviction, but on the contrary require submission to a rite that can be seen. The Baptist expression of the gospel is embodied in a form well adapted to the present.

Consequently Baptists challenge some odd but widespread Christian opinions. In the first place the claim is often heard that the question of which denomination to join is a matter of convenience, not of conviction. A believer, on this understanding, must take pains to learn the truths of salvation from the scriptures but need not trouble to explore how those truths impinge on the corporate existence of the church. The Bible, it is supposed, applies to the life of the individual but not to the life of the Christian community. Baptists, however, adopt a different stance. They want to proclaim biblical teaching about personal faith in Jesus Christ, but they notice that the Bible also contains guidance about how Christians should live together. Believers must be bound together in churches. It is actually rather strange to expect that the Bible should be concerned with the individual and not with the community. And any reader of the New Testament letters will realize that it is not so. Christians need to regulate their corporate life by the scriptures. That is what Baptist principles are about.

Another odd belief is that the exercise of authority among Christians ought to be restricted to a few. Yet that view is held, at least tacitly, by a majority of professing adherents of the faith. They hold that only a small body—whether bishops, presbyteries, or executive apostles—is qualified to lead. Even many who believe passionately in the application of democracy to political life often want to exclude most Christians from participation in crucial decision-making in the church. But Baptists see that Christ transforms human beings by giving them fresh insights. They are given an aptitude for participation in the government of the kingdom of God. That is often formulated as a belief in the priesthood of all believers. It would probably better be expressed as the kingship of all believers. Christians share in the kingly authority of Christ and so are qualified to join in the rule of his church. However it is put into words, Baptists want to insist that authority in the church rests ultimately with all the committed members. They have as inclusive a view of the ideal human society as anybody else.

A third oddity sometimes encountered among other Christians relates to the practice of baptism. Those who wish to defend the acceptance of infants for baptism commonly appeal to the Bible. Noticing that we are told that in certain respects there is a correspondence between New Testament baptism and Old Testament circumcision, they rush to the inference that the two rites ought to be administered to the same individuals. Since babies were once circumcised, they should now be baptized. But Baptists want to point out a fallacy in that argument. Under the old covenant, only male babies were baptized. If the case is valid that the subjects of baptism should be the same as the subjects of circumcision, then only boys should be baptized. The line of argument, though often heard, is extremely ill conceived. Baptists know that the visual symbol of baptism is powerful when the candidates are those who choose to be immersed out of personal conviction. Believer's baptism is the television of the gospel.

So a collection of sermons setting out Baptist distinctives is timely. On the one hand it speaks to our age; on the other it challenges conventional thinking among Christians. In a late nineteenth-century pamphlet entitled *The Duty of Baptists to Teach Their Distinctive Views*, the Southern Baptist theologian John A. Broadus declared that "it is not necessarily an arrogant or presumptuous thing in us if we strive to bring honored fellow-Christians to views which we honestly believe to be more scriptural, and therefore more wholesome." These sermons, while showing a similar respect for other believers, also commend Baptist faith and order with conviction.

David W. Bebbington, PhD
Professor of History, University of Stirling
Visiting Distinguished Professor of History, Baylor University

Introduction

For since in the wisdom of God the world by its wisdom did not know God, God was pleased to save those who believe by the foolishness of preaching. (1 Corinthians 1:21 NET)

Traditionally, church historians have marked 1609 as the year the first Baptist congregation in the world was founded. Thomas Helwys and a remnant of followers, who had earlier been a part of the English Separatist congregation led by John Smyth that had fled to Holland, returned to England to establish what most Baptists today celebrate as the first Baptist church. Over the course of the following centuries, Baptists would become known for holding distinctive Christian beliefs, while also sharing much of the core theology that makes them Protestant Christians.

As the Baptist tradition now begins its fifth century of existence, it joins other denominational traditions in attempting to maintain its identity in an increasingly "postdenominational" era. The postdenominational trend probably bodes well for its ecumenical openness, which might erase human-made boundaries that have separated Christians from one another in unhealthy and unproductive ways. However, it also has tended to mitigate the importance of distinctive church doctrine altogether, a trend that has abandoned Christian heritage, tradition, and established denominational distinctives in favor of shared contemporary congregational concerns for evangelism, discipleship, and the practical applications of the faith. Postmodern Christians are fearful that in becoming too distinctive as particular Christian entities, their churches will be isolated from the world around them.

Nevertheless, upon further reflection, one might readily see that it is for such a time as this that the distinctive Baptist tenets should not be sidelined but actually highlighted. For Baptists today, the environment of the post-Christendom world is not all that different from the one of their ancestors who followed Thomas Helwys and his little band to a homeland that rejected their beliefs. But instead of acquiescing to the world around them, Helwys and those Baptists who followed him forged ahead in carving out the distinctive Baptist witness. And four centuries of a faithful, missional, and evangelical Baptist Christianity have ensued. Now more than ever Baptists need to understand their past, not as family heirlooms viewed sentimentally on occasion but otherwise safely stored in their attic, but rather as an integral part of who they are today. Specifically, Baptists must recover and maintain their distinctive beliefs in order to reach the postmodern world for the gospel.

Nevertheless, this bold challenge, like most words of advice, is more easily said than done. In order to articulate that which is "distinctly Baptist," such tenets must first be identified. On first blush, this seems like a relatively easy task. After all, Baptists believe strongly in baptism by immersion, the priesthood of all believers, religious liberty, missions work, and the authority of the Scriptures. However, as surprising as this may seem to some readers, none of these convictions was original to Baptists! Additionally, Baptists are not by any stretch of the imagination the only tradition of Christians to hold any one of these beliefs. In fact, as one influential Baptist leader recently put it, "There's no single doctrine that is unique to Baptists, but their collective beliefs are distinctive. No other denomination holds this specific 'recipe' of convictions."[1] One of the two purposes of this book, then, is to outline what we Baptists believe to be our unique recipe. In doing so, we recognize the commonalities that we share with numerous other Christians, but we also celebrate the distinctive group of ingredients that make up the Baptist understanding of the faith.

Yet, to further complicate this project, an honest assessment of Baptist beliefs makes us recognize that not all Baptists have held to all of the tenets of any particular set of "distinctives." Indeed, one may find a Baptist group here and there that has objected to one or more of the tenets outlined in this book. Nevertheless, we have attempted to assemble fourteen principles that we believe to be distinctly Baptist—that is, principles held as basic beliefs maintained by most Baptists in most places throughout the world: the authority of Scripture, the necessity of coming to a personal conviction and confession of faith, the priesthood of all believers, the divine and ecclesial call to ministry, the importance of Christian mission, believer's baptism, the Lord's Supper, the voluntary membership of a believers' church, the ministry of social justice, soul competency, religious liberty, the autonomy of the local congregation, congregational church government, and the separation of church and state. Of course, we recognize that Baptists will differ with one another about the meaning of each of these distinctives. It is even probable that the contributors to this volume will disagree with one another regarding some emphases on various aspects of these distinctives. But most Baptists today and throughout our history agree in principle to these basic core convictions.

Baptist pastors typically learn about these convictions while in formal seminary training. Some laypeople might be fortunate enough to have experienced a short Sunday school series or special study on them. However, it seems that today fewer Baptists are aware of what makes their witness unique than has been the case in our past. Pastors and laypeople alike have grappled with how their fellow congregants might most easily learn about who they are and what they believe. And, although over the years, occasionally books are published and Sunday school lessons are written on this topic, it has been difficult to turn the tide of our own increasing ignorance of our own tradition and its tenets of faith.

Regardless, the pulpit continues to be the best place to educate a congregation and disseminate biblical knowledge to Christians. Like our fellow Protestants, Baptists have always seen preaching as central to our worship and congregational life. The great nineteenth-century British Baptist preacher Charles Haddon Spurgeon once remarked, "True preaching is an acceptable adoration of God by the manifestation of His gracious attributes: the testimony of His gospel . . . and the obedient hearing of revealed truth, are an acceptable form of worship of the Most High, and perhaps one of the most spiritual in which the human mind can be engaged."[2] Preaching, then, has been an essential means of teaching the core beliefs of Christianity to believers. Yet, pastors have struggled in the past to translate the doctrinal distinctives of their Baptist heritage learned in seminary courses into their proclamation and instruction from the pulpit of their churches. The predictable result has been the unfortunate ignorance on the part of their congregants regarding historic Baptist principles.

The idea of this book was developed by the faculty of the George W. Truett Theological Seminary at Baylor University in honor of the four hundredth anniversary of the founding of the Baptist tradition. Members of the faculty volunteered to pattern the proclamation of Baptist distinctives, initially as a chapel series at the seminary but culminating in the publication of its collected sermons. It is our hope that these sermons will inspire Baptists not only to hold onto our distinctive theology but also to inspire our pastors to continue to preach the Baptist understanding of our faith. This book might also be a useful study tool for laypersons outside the sanctuary in Bible studies, Sunday schools, midweek series, and individual study. In any event, this compilation represents our collective attempt to hand the faith down to future generations while informing the contemporary Baptist Christian of our tradition's valuable witness.

Of course, a concession is necessary regarding the publication of any sermon collection. Just as a letter or an e-mail fails to communicate on the level of a face-to-face conversation, Harry Emerson Fosdick once astutely observed that the essential nature of a sermon is such as to make it impossible for its printing to reproduce preaching. True preaching is always done in the context of Christian worship, and it requires the engagement both of listeners and preacher to be made effective. These sermons, then, serve merely as a record of that preaching event, somewhat assuaged by time and place and limited by the written word, without the help of its accompanying nonverbal expression, voice tonality, and the irreducible personality of each preacher. Nevertheless, the substance of what each proclaimer has attempted remains, for the most part, intact and will undoubtedly prove to be useful for clergy and laity alike.

As we celebrate the achievements of our Baptist ancestors these last four centuries, we recognize the challenge presented so eloquently by the preacher of the book of Hebrews: "Since we are surrounded by so great a cloud of witnesses, . . . let us run with perseverance the race that is set before us" (Hebrews 12:1). Our Baptist ancestors now hand to us the baton of the faith and the responsibility to bear its witness to our children, neighbors, and those in the far corners of the world. May this small book serve as a helpful tool for that enormous mission—"by the foolishness of preaching" (1 Corinthians 1:21).

Notes

1. Russell H. Dilday, *The Baylor Line*, December 2007, 6.
2. C. H. Spurgeon, *Lectures to My Students* (Grand Rapids: Zondervan, 1979), 53.

The Basics

Faith, Salvation, and the Scriptures

Faith and Salvation

A twelve-year-old boy became a Christian during a worship service. Later that week his friends at school began to ask him about his experience. "Did you see a vision?" one asked. "Did you hear God's voice?" asked another. The boy answered no to these questions. "Then, how did you know you were saved?" his friends finally asked. The boy searched for an answer, and finally he said, "It's like when you catch a fish. You can't see the fish or hear the fish; you just feel him tugging on your line. I just felt God tugging on my heart."[1]

Faith, one's trust in a person or thing, is an essential part of Christianity. The apostle Paul wrote, "We walk by faith, not by sight" (2 Corinthians 5:7). Christians always have emphasized that humans should place their trust in Jesus Christ, a person whom, after the first generation of Christians, no one on earth has seen in the flesh but whom Christians confess was and is the Son of God. Baptists, like many other Christians, have emphasized the need for each person to trust in the person and work of Jesus Christ for salvation. This individual emphasis is significant for Baptists, as they have underscored that no person is born Christian or made Christian by any ritual or ceremony. Additionally, no person can have proxy faith for another. Baptists believe, then, that Christian faith comes through a personal, individual conversion by God's grace through repentance and belief. But as Dennis Tucker notes in his sermon on salvation to follow, faith is not merely an assent to a set of truth claims, however compelling those may be. One finds faith in Christ Jesus and its resulting salvation by identifying with his life, death, and resurrection. Thus, a Christian is someone who not only believes with the mind but also acts out this belief in life, heeding Christ's call to all who want to be among his followers: "Let them deny themselves and take up their cross daily and follow me" (Luke 9:23). Genuine faith, then, produces heartfelt love for God and neighbor and service to those around each Christian because of such love. This is not, however, to say that salvation comes as a combination of faith and human works. Instead, the faithful works of each Christian come as the genuine fruit of the faith given by Christ. As James writes, "Be doers of the word, and not merely hearers who deceive themselves. ... So faith by itself, if it has no works, is dead" (James 1:22; 2:17).

The Scriptures

But Baptists believe that faith is inextricably connected to the Scriptures. The revelation of God and the understanding of the faith are the purposes of Scripture. John Smyth wrote in 1608, "The matter or substance of the scripture hath in it, Logick, History, Cronology, Cosmography, Genealogy, Philosophy, Theologie & other like matter. The principall parte of the matter is the Theologie."[2] Yet this understanding of "theologie" was not intended to mean a merely cerebral and pedantic approach to the Scriptures. The 1963 *Baptist Faith and Message* observes,

> Baptists are a people who profess a living faith. This faith is rooted and grounded in Jesus Christ who is 'the same yesterday, and to-day, and for ever.' Therefore, the sole authority for faith and practice among Baptists is Jesus Christ whose will is revealed in the Holy Scriptures.[3]

The Scriptures, like the appropriation of the faith, are to be understood as the guide for following Christ, both in word and in deed, both in theology and in ethics. Baptists believe that the way every Christian comes to know about Christ Jesus is through God's written word, the Scriptures of the Old and New Testaments. This knowledge may be presented through sermons, tracts, books, classes, television and radio programs, and personal conversations, but a true knowledge of Christian faith is always based upon these same Scriptures, which comprise the Bible. The Bible is God's written, authoritative word, normative for Christian faith and practice. Baptists, like many other Protestants, believe that the Bible stands above every tradition, and all confessions and traditions must be measured by Scripture. The proclamation of the Christian faith must be rooted in and governed by the Bible.

Additionally, the Scriptures give guidance for how each individual and Christian community is intended to live. M. E. Dodd remarks,

"One distinguishing characteristic of Baptists through the centuries has been their absolute allegiance and unflinching loyalty to the Scriptures. It has been their age long contention that the Bible and the Bible alone could be accepted as an unerring rule of faith and practice."[4] While the Bible points Christians to Jesus Christ and admonishes Christians to live in Christlike ways, the Scriptures too are likewise interpreted through the lens of Jesus. The 1963 *Baptist Faith and Message* affirms that "the criterion by which the Bible is to be interpreted is Jesus Christ." This is to say that the Bible is essentially about Jesus and is understood by way of his life, teachings, ministry, death, and resurrection as the Scriptures record it.

At the same time, as Roger Olson notes in his sermon on the Bible to follow, the Scriptures are less about information than transformation. The Scriptures were intended to change the lives of those who read or hear them. As Dwight L. Moody said, "The Scriptures were not given to increase our knowledge but to change our lives." Through the Bible, humans come to learn that they are sinners separated from God, and they come to understand also that Christ Jesus died and rose again to defeat their sin, save them from sin's eternal punishment, and grant them, through faith, the inheritance of an undeserved, eternal reward and reunion with God. Such knowledge, when inspired by the Holy Spirit, guides each person not only to believe but also to live in service to God and others. Thus, salvation comes, Baptists believe, by the Holy Spirit through the hearing of the written word and through the living faith that it produces in each person.

Notes

1. "How You Know," in *Illustrations Unlimited*, ed. James S. Hewitt (Wheaton, IL: Tyndale House, 1988), 188.
2. John Smyth, "Differences of the Churches of the Separation," cited in H. Leon McBeth, *A Sourcebook for Baptist Heritage* (Nashville: B&H Academic, 1990), 16.
3. *The Baptist Faith and Message* (Nashville: Sunday School Board of the Southern Baptist Convention, 1963), 5.
4. M. E. Dodd, *Baptist Principles and Practices* (Alexandria, LA: Chronicle Publishing, 1916), 8.

Action Steps for the Reader

1. For further reading on faith and the Scriptures:

Augustine. *On Christian Belief.* Hyde Park, NY: New City Press, 2005.

Fee, Gordon D., and Douglas Stuart. *How to Read the Bible for All Its Worth: A Guide to Understanding the Bible.* Grand Rapids: Zondervan, 1991.

Green, E. M. B. *The Meaning of Salvation.* Philadelphia: Westminster, 1965.

James, Robison B., ed. *The Unfettered Word: Confronting the Authority-Inerrancy Question.* Macon, GA: Smyth & Helwys, 1994.

Johnson, Luke Timothy. *Scripture and Discernment: Decision Making in the Church.* Nashville: Abingdon, 1983.

Luther, Martin. "Two Kinds of Righteousness." In vol. 31 of *Luther's Works,* ed. Harold Grimm, 297–306. Philadelphia: Fortress, 1957.

Wright, N. T. *Scripture and the Authority of God.* London: SPCK, 2005.

2. Biblical texts for preaching and topical Bible study:

Faith and salvation: Psalm 62:1-7; 98:1-3; Isaiah 12:1-3; John 3:14-18,36; 5:24; Romans 4; 10:1-13; 1 Corinthians 1:18-19; Ephesians 2:1-10; 1 Timothy 2:1-6; James 1:19-27; 2:14-26; Hebrews 2:3-10; 1 Peter 1:1-10.

The Scriptures: Matthew 22:23-33; Luke 24:25-27; Acts 8:26-35; 1 Timothy 4:9-13; 2 Timothy 3:14-17; 2 Peter 1:16-21.

3. Idea for worship:

For the Scripture reading in worship, occasionally use a reading group to read the lines of various characters in a passage to help make it more fresh and alive.

4. Opportunity for service:

Do a service project with your church that involves donating or sharing Bibles with those who need them (e.g., in cooperation with the Gideons International, Wycliffe Bible Translators, American Bible Society, or your denominational or state missions board).

CHAPTER 1

A SERMON ON THE BAPTIST DISTINCTIVE OF
Salvation

"But God Made Us Alive Together with Christ"

W. DENNIS TUCKER JR.

Ephesians 2:1-10

I n his reflections on the topic of salvation, Brad Creed, former dean of Truett Seminary and now provost at Samford University, returned to images from his childhood experiences. He says that in the Baptist churches where he grew up, "the burden of being Baptist . . . return[ed] repeatedly to the subject of salvation."[1] And then he explains,

> We were keenly aware of those among us who had and had not made professions of faith. For those of us who had not, we approached the semiannual revival meetings with both longing and dread. This could be the year when those who had not yet made professions of faith might be saved. The evangelists who held the meetings were spellbinding, impassioned orators. With mere words fervently spoken, they opened the glories of heaven to the listeners and drew us into the stark gravity and sobering reality of human sinfulness. When they preached of the judgment awaiting the lost, hell was so hot you could feel the flames licking at your heels. Even after I had made my profession of faith and knew that my salvation was secure, I gripped the back of the pew during the invitation time of those revival meetings until my knuckles turned white. . . . These revivals were main events in the Baptist life of my childhood and youth. All other local church events throughout the year were either preamble or postlude.[2]

And so it is that perhaps some of you grew up in churches where you too attended such white-knuckled, pew-grabbing, flame-licking, judgment-preaching events. But my hunch is that most of us did not. Although Creed offers a somewhat comical depiction of the event, he seems to suggest that the revival was central apparently because it was there—especially there—that issues of salvation rose to the fore. Salvation was a decision to be made that night, in that church, at the close of that service. Your life was in the balance; salvation was at stake.

In a much earlier generation of Baptists, these same kinds of meetings proved most formative in the life of George W. Truett as well. Truett alluded to the many sermons he heard during his early life that spoke of "Christ and his great salvation." But it was not until he was nineteen years old that he made a decision. Truett recounts one service in the Baptist County Church House in Clay County, North Carolina:

> When the preacher concluded his sermon, with the ringing challenge for immediate and unreserved acceptance of Christ as a personal Saviour, a large number promptly went forward, publicly professing Christ before all the people. I was glad to be in that number. I could "draw back" no longer from such public commitment and confession.[3]

As I read through Truett's biography, it was clear that these sermons preached in rural churches scattered in the foothills of North Carolina had in some way opened his eyes and heart to the gospel of Jesus, to the point that he no could longer "draw back" from such commitment and confession.

In preparing for this series, however, I read an article in which Charles Cousar laments that salvation as a term is rarely heard in sermons these days. Unlike Truett and Creed, who often heard the term *salvation* and sermons on salvation, Cousar rarely hears such a sermon any more. He proffers a guess as to the rationale: "It may conjure up too many recollections of old-time revivals, when people 'got saved,' if only for a short spell. Apparently a moratorium of sorts has fallen on the use of the term, at least in mainline churches."[4] Perhaps the term has become passé. Perhaps we fear that it is neither politically correct nor practically relevant anymore. Perhaps the sermons of some have moved on to what are perceived as more culturally relevant issues, or at least more culturally palatable issues for our congregants.

Historically for Baptists, however, salvation stands at the core of their identity. Obviously, the confession "Jesus saves" is not uniquely that of the Baptist tradition, but Baptists have and remain "conversionists in their understanding of the need for personal response to God's love and grace."[5] Therefore, it is fitting in a series devoted to Baptist distinctives that we begin with a focus on the Christian faith, and in particular, salvation through Jesus Christ.

It seems that before we can speak of the priesthood of all believers, before we can talk about soul competency, believers' church, or the autonomy of the local church, we must speak of salvation. And the reason is simple: it is our shared confession in the risen Christ and our vision of a shared life in the resurrected one that call us to live in community in this tradition that we call "Baptist."

The book of Ephesians returns us to this issue and calls us to turn our thoughts to that of salvation and its implications. Paul reminds the community gathered at Ephesus about the shared confession concerning salvation, and more than simply being a statement of doctrine, this reminder becomes a call for faithful living.

The Plight of Us All

In Ephesians 2:1-3 Paul reminds us of the plight that befalls all of us. Following a tightly constructed prayer in 1:15-23, in which he celebrates the resurrection and glorification of Jesus, who is "above every name that is named, not only in this age but also in the age to come" (v. 21), Paul pivots in 2:1 to say, "And *you*. . . ." He turns from the work of God in Christ to ask, "And *you*—what of the work of God in *you* through Christ?"

Paul rarely minces words, and he does not do so here. Paul's description of the human condition leaves little to the imagination. The opening three verses explode with images, piling up descriptions of life apart from Christ. He tells his readers that they were like corpses, "dead through trespasses and sins" (2:1). They were like slaves, "following the course of this world, following the prince of the power of the air, the spirit that is now at work among those who are disobedient" (2:2). The Greek word behind "course" (*aiōn*) might better be translated as "age." In essence, apart from Christ, we are forever slaves to the age of this world. Those who are slaves of this world know nothing of the new age, of the new course announced in the life, death, and resurrection of Jesus.

But then notice the subtle shift in pronouns in 2:3. Paul says, "All of *us* once lived among them in the passions of *our* flesh, . . . and *we* were by nature children of wrath." Paul knows that this is a shared confession. Paul not only knows this shared confession, but also he is not afraid to speak of it. But such a confession is not made easily these days. For most people, the word *sin*, like *salvation*, is not readily discussed.

In his book *The Light Within You*, John Claypool notes the ambivalent attitude toward sin present today. Claypool cites a noted British psychologist who states that modern humans "are no longer troubled about their sins. They regard this category as a hangover from a primitive past. They have outgrown such a concept."[6]

And perhaps it is not just modern humankind in general that has deluded itself into believing that it can outgrow the concept of sin; maybe even many Christians have convinced themselves that human sinfulness is the stuff of antiquated tent revivals and zealous Christians from a bygone era.

Yet, Paul calls us back to the reality of sin: apart from Christ, we are in fact nothing more than a corpse bound to a way of life shaped by a system that does not consider God.[7] And Paul reminds us: *that* is his confession, *that* is their confession, and *that* is our confession; each and every one of us is part of the "we" he proclaims in 2:3. Paul reminds us that apart from Christ, we are that corpse. Apart from Christ, we are that slave. Apart from Christ, we know nothing of this new age, this new course, this new life bound up with Christ.

But God . . .

What proves striking in this text, however, is that Paul does not mention our helpless state in order to shame us or, more generally, to reject the value of humanity. To the contrary, Paul affirms our value by suggesting that despite our corpse-ridden, slave-driven state, God refuses to stay out of the picture.

In 2:4 Paul pivots again to say, "But God . . . ." When all seems lost, when it seems that there is no hope, Paul says, "But God . . . ." This phrase breaks in, shifting our thoughts from a humanity that lacks everything to a God who has everything, a God who is "rich in mercy." And despite the fact that all of us once lived in the passions of our flesh and followed the course of this world, Paul emphatically declares, God steps in "out of the great love with which he loved us." Paul even said in 2:3 that we were "children of the wrath." But in 2:4 he proclaims that the children of wrath encountered not wrath, but God and "the great love with which he loved us." And it is this great love that made us alive "with Christ," raised us up "with Christ," and made us sit "with Christ" in the heavenly places. As one writer explains, "Faith has an adhesive quality to it; it binds the believer to the one who is believed."[8]

In many churches, we have equated faith with assent to a set of claims or the teachings that one affirms, and so we frequently speak of "the Christian faith." But in Ephesians, faith is unqualified solidarity with the one who loved us out of his richness. It is this solidarity with Christ, who made us alive, raised us up, and gave us a place to sit that changes the now for all of us.

Further, this solidarity, this life with Christ, also says something about our life with one another. If each person who follows Christ is in effect "with Christ," then likewise all of us share life together because we are all "with Christ" together. This is expressed clearly in 2:5, where Paul says that God "made us alive together with Christ."

This notion is reflected in Dietrich Bonhoeffer's *Life Together*, in which he writes, "Christian [community] is not an ideal in which we must realize, it is rather a reality created by God *in Christ* in which we may participate."[9]

Such an understanding has enormous implications for how Baptist ecclesiology has expressed itself. Noted Baptist historian Karen Smith explains, "The basis of Baptist life has always been that the believers are never alone, but bound together"; and further, as our text suggests, they are bound together "with Christ."[10] Thus, we are a church because we are a gathered community comprised of individuals who were saved by grace through faith, yet who understand that we have been made alive together with Christ for the living of these days.

Our community is a result of our salvation. Our salvation and our community with Christ and with one another is not our own doing; it is the gift of God.

Participating in the New Creation

The final verse in this passage describes what living in these days should look like. Paul writes, "For we are what he has made us, created in Christ Jesus for good works, which God prepared beforehand to be our way of life" (2:10). This translation (NRSV) partly misses the subtle play on words in this text. In the Greek, the first phrase might be more aptly translated as "for we are his work." The Greek word for "work" (*poiēma*) is used in the Septuagint to refer to God's creation, and here Paul picks up that same word here to suggest we are a new work, a new creation through God. The implication is that through salvation we have been changed. To pretend that we have not is to miss what it means to have been created anew in Christ Jesus.

Early Baptists understood something of what it means to be changed fully in Christ Jesus. Because they felt they were in fact new creations in Christ Jesus and hence new works of God, they sometimes had their names changed. And so Praise-God Barebone was a pastor of a small church in England around 1640. He was joined by his two brothers, "Christ-came-into-the-world-to-save Barebone" and the somewhat more radical "If-Christ-had-not-died-thou-hadst-been damned Barebone."[11] Obviously, today such names would be tough to squeeze onto a business card or work into an e-mail address, but for them, they knew to their core that they were not who they had been. They were now new works of God.

Salvation has, in many ways, become so perfunctory that perhaps we have forgotten the full measure of what has happened in Christ Jesus. Perhaps when we simply say, "I have been saved," we allow ourselves to forget the implications of that statement. Yes, we have been delivered from something; but much more, we have been made anew into the handiwork of Christ Jesus. We have been changed fully.

But what is the purpose of this new creation? Paul states that we were created in Christ Jesus "for good works." In this clause, the Greek word for "work" (*ergon*) implies deeds or actions. Now, any good Baptist gets nervous any time the word *works* appears in the same sermon with *salvation*. But here we have them both, and they are inseparable. Paul announces that we are the work of God created to do the work of God.

Recently, as I was taking my dog to the veterinarian, I passed a local church. Out front was a sign that read, "America, a great place to live while waiting for heaven." I actually turned around and went back to make sure that I had read the sign correctly: "America, a great place to live while waiting for heaven." Since when has salvation meant that we wait for heaven? Is salvation nothing more than an invitation to fly in a holding pattern until a new day?

Our text in Ephesians says explicitly that those who have tasted salvation do not have to wait for the day of a new creation, because they themselves are the new creation, created in Christ Jesus to do his good works. The expectation for a new day, the expectation for a new creation, is lived out in the now, for we are that new creation. And if we are the new creation of God in this divine now, how can we shirk doing the good works of Christ Jesus?

A hymn was composed in the late 1800s for the Baptist Missionary Society. The hymn was meant specifically to call Christian women to the foreign fields for missions. The first verse says,

O Women-hearts, that keep the days of old,
In living memory, can you stand back
When Christ calls? . . .
Do you forget the Hand that placed the Crown
Of Happy freedom on the Woman's head,
And took her from the dying and the dead,
Lifting the wounded soul, long trodden down?[12]

How can we stand back when Christ calls us to action, the hymn writer asks. In part, it is this sense of being called to do the work of Christ that has prompted the missiological commitments of Baptists. In part, it is this sense of being called to be the new creation and to participate in bringing about this new age that has prompted Baptists

in their commitments to social justice. Salvation stands at the center
of all that we do, not simply because we can claim that we are saved,
but because, as a new creation, it shapes all that we are to become.

If we know something of the salvation to which Paul refers, then
we cannot stand back when Christ calls. If we know something of
the salvation to which Paul refers, then we know we are not who we
once were. And if we know something of this salvation, then we
must know what it means to be Christ's work set aside to do his
good work.

Notes

1. J. Bradley Creed, "Salvation," in *A Baptist's Theology*, ed. R. Wayne
   Stacy (Macon, GA: Smyth & Helwys, 1999), 102.
2. Ibid.
3. Powhatan W. James, *George W. Truett: A Biography* (Nashville: Broad-
   man, 1953), 24.
4. Walter Brueggemann et al., *Texts for Preaching: A Lectionary Commentary Based on the NRSV, Year B* (Louisville: Westminster John
   Knox, 1993), 225.
5. Bill J. Leonard, *Baptist Ways: A History* (Valley Forge, PA: Judson Press,
   2003), 3.
6. John Claypool, *The Light Within You* (Waco, TX: Word, 1983), 183.
7. Klyne Snodgrass, *Ephesians*, NIV Application Commentary (Grand
   Rapids: Zondervan, 1996), 96.
8. Ibid., 105.
9. Dietrich Bonhoeffer, *Life Together*, trans. John W. Doberstein (New
   York: Harper, 1954), 30 (italics added).
10. Karen Smith, "The Covenant Life of Some Eighteenth-Century Calvin-
    istic Baptists in Hampshire and Wiltshire," in *Pilgrim Pathways: Essays
    in Baptist History in Honour of B. R. White*, ed. William H. Brackney
    and Paul S. Fiddes, with John H. Y. Briggs (Macon, GA: Mercer Univer-
    sity Press, 1999), 165.
11. Leonard, *Baptist Ways*, 30.
12. Ibid., 150.

CHAPTER 2

A SERMON ON THE BAPTIST DISTINCTIVE OF THE
Authority of Scripture

The Baptist View of the Bible

ROGER E. OLSON
2 Timothy 3:16

Almost everyone knows something about the Bible, and all of us approach it with baggage. Of course, I do not mean literal baggage, as in "luggage," but baggage as in preconceived notions. To some people, the Bible is a threat to their personal liberty; to others, it is a manuscript from heaven written by God himself. Everyone thinks something about the Bible, whether they have read it or not.

My Bible baggage stems from my childhood and youth, when a favored Sunday school song, sung also in vacation Bible school, was "The B-I-B-L-E" ("Yes, that's the book for me!"). I remember singing that song with my peers and picturing myself standing on a Bible, which was anathema in my home and church! You see, a line in the ditty says, "I stand alone on the Word of God." That word "alone" also stuck with me; it gave me the impression that each Christian had a unique personal relationship with the Bible apart from everyone else.

Of course, that is not what the unknown songwriter intended; the "alone" is supposed to describe the Bible's supreme authority over every other book. But to my childish mind it designated the individual's use of the Bible. You see, we did not read the Bible aloud in church; in our church a preacher delivered a stirring sermon based on a passage in the Bible, but we did not have the customary reading of "lessons" from the Old and New Testaments as part of public worship. Instead, we read the Bible devotionally and usually alone. So, like many other Christians, I developed Bible baggage about the Bible being God's written word to me, and what it meant was what it meant to me as God spoke directly to me through it.

I now realize, partly as a result of my seminary education, that much of my childhood Bible baggage was defective; it needed to be repaired without being thrown out entirely. As the old saying goes, "Don't throw the baby out with the bathwater." So I have tried to learn to throw out the individualistic approach to the Bible while retaining certain other aspects of my youthful relationship with it.

There was one other facet of my childhood Bible baggage that I had to overcome: a tendency to worship the Bible. In my church and home it was considered sacrilegious to put anything on top of the Bible. If I came home from school and happened accidently to lay a textbook on top of a Bible (and there were many Bibles around our house), my mother would sternly lecture me about that and make me remove the offending book immediately.

Later, again as part of my seminary experience, I learned about "bibliolatry," an idolatry of the paper and ink and leather of the Bible. But I also learned that bibliolatry extends to any treatment of the Bible as functionally equal with God. I realized that my childhood church and home tended to treat the Bible as the fourth member of the Trinity, and that this was wrong.

You might wonder if there was anything to celebrate about my childhood experience of the Bible. Absolutely there is. It is best described by a phrase coined by Yale Divinity School theologian Hans Frei, a very important Protestant theologian of the second half of the twentieth century. Frei said that for the Christian, "the Bible absorbs the world."

Now, for many people that is an enigmatic statement, a true head-scratcher. But the first time I read it, I knew what Frei meant, because it describes perfectly what I experienced as a child growing up in a very Bible-centered church and home. Here I am not talking about the individualistic approach to the Bible or our unconscious bibliolatry; rather, I am talking about our love of the Bible and our practice of seeing the whole world through its story of God's love.

When we viewed the world around us we automatically saw it as created by God, corrupted by sin, and redeemed by God through the life, death, and resurrection of Jesus Christ. For us, the Bible was a great "theodrama" that explained everything really important. Of course, we did not think that the Bible told us which car to buy, but it did tell us not to be attached to a car or any other material possession.

Baptists disagree about the doctrine of the Bible. We often engage in battles over the Bible because of our differing interpretations of the doctrine of Scripture. Some Baptists insist that the Bible must be inerrant, while others say that it is infallible but not inerrant. Some even dismiss its supernatural verbal inspiration, calling that belief a subtle form of bibliolatry. Baptists are all over the theological landscape when it comes to beliefs about the Bible, but we all agree that the Bible should absorb the world for us.

We are all "people of the book" even as we debate the book's attributes. What binds us together about the Bible is its power to shape our lives in the world and our love for it. We may and do disagree about its precise nature, but we agree about its life-transforming power and its centrality to all of life.

In practical terms, that means much more than having an open Bible on the altar of the church and insisting that every Sunday school class study the Bible. In practice, that we are people of the book means that we immerse ourselves in the Bible—its stories, poetry, wisdom, and teachings. We memorize large portions of it, but more importantly we strive to find ourselves in its story of God and his people.

Four Claims about Our View of the Bible

Because of this bedrock view of the Bible and the practice that it encourages, Baptists traditionally have made four major claims about the Bible itself on the basis of our experience of it as God's story and ours.

First, as people of the book, we say the Bible is *the* inspired and authoritative word of God. In other words, it is God's message in human words; like Jesus himself, it has two natures, divine and human. Of course, we do not (or at least should not) put it on the same plane as Jesus, who is God incarnate. The Bible is a book; it is not God. It expresses much about God to us, but it is not really God as Jesus is God. But we do believe that it has a divine aspect in that it brings God's word, God's message of creation and redemption, to us. It has power to draw us into encounter with God and communicate God's message to us as no other book does. In this regard, it is unique among books.

When it comes to spiritual matters pertaining to knowing God and having a right relationship with him, Baptists turn to the Bible first and foremost and are rightly suspicious of other sources that claim equal power to communicate God and create spiritual life. We believe, with the great Reformers of the church, that the Bible and the Holy Spirit are bound inseparably together; the Spirit inspired and illumines the Bible to our hearts and minds and convinces us that it is God's unique word. Without the Spirit, the Bible would be a dead letter, unable to prompt and guide spiritual life. But the Spirit is bound to the Bible; outside the Bible, the Spirit does not speak authoritative truth necessary for salvation and Christian life.

Second, as people of the book, we say that the Bible is not an esoteric book, but rather is open to every Christian equally. While we recognize the value of biblical scholars to help us understand the written word, we do not acknowledge any special spiritual class of people especially capable of reading and interpreting the Bible just because of who they are. Education helps, but ordination alone does not. All Christians in the pews, not just those in pulpits, can and should read the Bible and enter into lively conversation with it. That does not mean that everyone's interpretation is equally true, but it does means that nobody's interpretation is privileged by reason of the interpreter belonging to a certain class or group.

Third, as people of the book, we insist that no human creed or doctrinal statement stands above or even alongside Scripture in terms of authority for faith and life. We respect early church creeds such as the Apostles' Creed and the Nicene Creed, and occasionally we write doctrinal statements that explain what we believe. But none of these are sacrosanct or immutable. They are open to revision as newer and better faithful scholarship sheds new light on Scripture's meaning. And none of them affords the new life in Christ that we experience through the message of Scripture itself.

Fourth, as people of the book we traditionally have found Jesus Christ to be the key to interpreting Scripture. As Martin Luther said, and as we discover in our encounter with it, the Bible is the cradle that brings us the Christ child. In other words, the Bible has a focus, and it is not anything and everything; it is the person of Jesus Christ. We believe the Bible because it communicates Christ to us; we do not believe in Christ because he is in the Bible. We are indeed people of the book, but even more, we are Jesus people. And we are people of the book because we are Jesus people.

An old saying has it that you can make the Bible mean anything you want it to, but there is a way to avoid that, and Baptists traditionally have followed that way. We view the whole Bible through the lens of God with us in Jesus Christ. It is a book about him even though it contains much that does not seem on the surface to be that. It is not that we play games—for instance, finding Jesus hidden in the Old Testament tabernacle and its furniture. Rather, we find the inner meaning of the biblical narrative as leading up to Jesus Christ—his first coming, his being with us in the interim, and his return.

Four Corrections about Our View of the Bible

Having looked at the Baptist ethos about the Bible, we turn in another direction to some words of correction in four parts. Baptists sometimes forget their own heritage and its basic beliefs and practices and need to be reminded of them. And in each generation new challenges arise that call forth new correctives. Here I offer four statements that I hope will help call Baptists back to a proper view of the Bible whenever they start to stray away from it.

First, the purpose of Scripture is not information, but transformation. We are experiential Christians; for us, experiencing God is more important than anything else, and by "experiencing" we mean "being transformed." We know that we are sinners in need of redemption, but sometimes we subvert that knowledge by focusing too much on facts. True, facts and values cannot be entirely separated, but the real purpose of Scripture (and of the Holy Spirit speaking Jesus Christ into our lives through it) is not to fill our heads with facts but to transform our lives.

Baptist battles over the Bible too often have been about the factual status of the Bible. All of us agree that the Bible is true, but we must remember that its truth is not limited to communication of factual knowledge. We say with Scripture that Jesus Christ is "the way, and the truth, and the life" (John 14:6). But how can a person *be* truth if truth is merely facts? That Jesus is the truth means, in a way unparalleled by anyone else, that he redeems us and shapes us into godly persons. By all means, we must acknowledge that facts play a role in this, but some people, including some Baptists, place too much emphasis on facts, as if they were the be-all and end-all of revelation. They are not.

Second, the Bible's power to communicate God to us and draw us into the true story of God and his people is not magical, but sacramental. I realize some Baptists recoil in horror at the word *sacrament*. They should not. It simply refers to any means of grace. Surely the Bible is a means of grace, but not in a magical way. (We should not allow the good word *sacrament* to become a synonym for *magic*, even though some Christians tend to treat them as the same.) Magic is any way of manipulating God (or the forces of nature) to do something. It treats things that are not objects as objects.

For example, while the Bible as paper, ink, and leather is an object, the word of God is not an object. It cannot be manipulated. Word of God and grace are inextricably united, and certainly grace cannot be compelled. However, some well-intentioned but misguided Baptists (and others, to be sure) treat the Bible as if it were a magical talisman that automatically emits a gracious energy or automatically communicates transforming grace into our lives.

A Baptist contractor hid Bibles inside the walls of houses that he was building expecting their very presence, unknown to the occupants, to emit a spiritual aura that would begin to change lives. A Baptist teacher sought guidance from God by simply dropping open the Bible and pointing randomly to verses and trying to interpret them as daily "marching orders" for her life. These are magical practices that would turn the Bible into a charm, when really it is a sacrament of God's transforming power. It is indeed a channel of grace, but not automatically. It has to be read or heard and interpreted for grace to come through it. The grace is in the meaning, not in the paper, ink, and leather.

Third, the practice of Scripture is not mechanical, but imaginative. As one contemporary evangelical theologian has put it, we are not called to "stare at" the Bible but rather to "look along it." The Bible is not like an old recipe book handed down from generation to generation and followed slavishly. It is more like a compass or a sight on a rifle; it points in the right direction.

Another evangelical theologian has said the Bible is like two acts of a three-act play where the third act is to be improvised on the basis of the first two acts. We, God's people, are the actors who must faithfully improvise, in our own cultural context, the third act. That calls for imagination rooted in thorough acquaintance with the first two acts.

Unfortunately, some Baptists (and others, of course) tend to think that faithfulness to the Bible is staring at it and never using their imaginations to apply it to new situations. By "imagination" I do not mean pretending. Here "imagination" means creative application of something to a different situation. At their best, Baptists are people who know the Bible's story so thoroughly that they are able creatively to continue the story two thousand years later and in entirely different cultural contexts.

Fourth, the right place of Scripture is not in the individual's solitude but in the community of God's people. This is what I had to learn after being led as a child to believe that the Bible is primarily for individual devotional reading. Baptists have become too individualistic; that is part of our accommodation to culture. So we tend to think that the Bible is for individual consumption, interpretation, and application. I know of Baptists who resist any appeal to explain their interpretation of the Bible, not because they are uncertain about it, but because they think that it is private.

The privatization of Scripture is the bane of modern Christianity, and it was entirely foreign to ancient Christianity. The earliest Christians clearly read Scripture (the prophets and writings of the apostles) together and submitted their interpretations for examination to each other in community.

Too often we have taken the Bible out of the church and put it too exclusively in the private sphere of individual spirituality. It was never meant to be there. At their best, Baptists are not only people of the book, but also people of the church. So important is the church to

Christian living that Paul equates the church with Christ (1 Corinthians 12:12,27; Ephesians 4:12). Of course, this is clearly a figure of speech, a metonym. A modern example is when a reporter declares, "The White House said today . . . ." The White House does not literally say anything; in this situation the phrase "White House" is being used for someone in the White House, either the president or a spokesperson for the president.

The Bible is never said to be Christ, but that notion is used of the church, and it says something important about the church: it is closely tied to Jesus himself. As we know from the New Testament, the church is his body. Surely that should tell us that Scripture belongs first and foremost to the church, and the individual's use of the Bible should be guided by Christ through his church.

This does not mean that an individual can never speak a word of correction to the church based on a personal reading of Scripture. Luther did that, and we are grateful that he did. But Luther never saw himself as a mountaintop guru descending to cast aspersions on the church from outside of it. He set out to reform the church, and in doing so he read the Bible along with the church fathers and for the sake of the church.

The Baptist view of the Bible is complicated; where two or three Baptists are gathered, there we will find two or three different views of the Bible. There is no Baptist pope to compel agreement. But what I have tried to do here is present a Baptist consensus about the Bible and some words of correction for those Baptists (and others) who tend to stray away from its true purpose and use.

Christian Responsibility

Soul Competency, the Priesthood of All Believers, Social Justice, and Christian Mission

Soul Competency

That Baptists understand the faith not only through the community of the church but also through their individual acceptance of the faith was discussed in the preceding section. However, this dual role of individual and community faith is essential for understanding the four Baptist distinctives and the respective sermons that comprise this section.

Baptists understand that those who follow Jesus have special privileges because of this divine-human relationship, but also special duties incumbent upon each person. Soul competency, the priesthood of all believers, social justice, and Christian mission are concepts familiar to most Baptists. But to have a healthy and balanced understanding of each of these Baptist tenets, one must see that with each spiritual duty comes opportunity, with each spiritual privilege comes accountability.

Because Baptists emphasize that the Christian faith must be personally appropriated by each individual, it follows for them that each person is singularly accountable before God. Thus, Baptist historian H. Leon McBeth notes that this distinctive "means that God has endowed every person with the ability to decide—and not only the power to decide, but also the necessity to decide," while rightly noting that "soul competency is not a human achievement; it is an endowment from God who created us."[1] Often this concept is understood positively as a dispensation or right celebrated by each person. For instance, W. R. White wrote along these lines that

> the individual is of priceless value [to God]. No building, work of art, human or religious institution is to be valued above him. They, like the Sabbath, are made for him, and not he for them. . . . We hold that the individual is endowed with the alienable right to worship or not worship God according to the dictates of his conscience and the right of free choice. We believe that this right is irrevocable and must be kept inviolate. . . . The individual has a right to express his religious or antireligious convictions. Otherwise, freedom is only half born.[2]

The freedom for each person to choose God and voluntarily appropriate the faith is a basic principle of Baptist beliefs. However, as David Garland notes in the sermon on this topic to follow, soul competency "assumes that God allows human beings to make choices, and that they are held accountable for their choices." The second part of this assumption comes as a sobering reminder that each person will also be held responsible for his or her choices in faith by God. And Baptists historically have emphasized this serious notion as one for which every human one day will be judged by God. Thus, the freedom of soul competency must never be separated from individual responsibility.

The Priesthood of All Believers

The same counterpoise must be used in describing the Protestant notion of the priesthood of all believers, which Baptists have always held tenaciously. When he first posited this Protestant doctrine in the sixteenth century, Martin Luther, often called the "father of the Reformation," argued that a Christian is both "the most free lord of all, and subject to none" while also "the most dutiful servant of all, and subject to every one." Patterning this concept from Paul's description of Christ in Philippians 2:1-11 and Peter's description of church as "a holy priesthood" (1 Peter 2:5), Luther understood Christians as "worthy to appear before God, to pray for others, and to teach one another" the things of God. Thus, like the Baptist understanding of soul competency, the Protestant notion of the priesthood of all believers maintains the tension of divine honor and humble responsibility, which each Christian must balance. Baptist theologian James Leo Garrett observes, "Despite modern denials by certain Baptists that Baptists are Protestants, the matrix of the Baptist movement has been powerfully shaped by the Protestant Reformation, and some have even claimed that the Baptists are the truly thoroughgoing Reformers."[3] Regardless, Baptists share with other Protestants some notion of an egalitarian priesthood of all Christians. However, this theological shift from ecclesial hierarchy must be understood rightly. Baptist historian Robert G. Torbet once remarked that the Protestant Reformation sought less to "unfrock the clergy as it ordained the laity."[4]

By virtue of one's baptism, the confessing Christian is made a priest, one who stands directly before God, has direct and equal access to God, and can pray to God without the need of any human intermediary. As a priest, each individual is granted the right to voice convictions within the church, interpret Scripture for personal living, and lead a life of devotion to God. Nevertheless, as Joel Gregory demonstrates in his sermon on this topic to follow, such a benefit is not to be understood as making the Christian a kind of Lone Ranger without need of fellowship, Christian reproof, corporate worship, and selfless service to others. A Christian may well be a "most free lord," but a Christian is also a "most dutiful servant" to others. Paradoxically, one compels the other! A priest not only has a high standing, but also bears a weighty obligation to pray for, minister to, and serve neighbors.

Such a concept necessitates a balance not only within the individual Christian, but also in the roles of the laity and the clergy. Baptists do not interpret the priesthood of all believers so radically that they, in Quaker fashion, have dissolved the clergy. Instead, as British Baptist Nigel Wright puts it, the church encompasses the "leadership of some and the ministry of all."[5] In other words, the clergy are those who, on behalf of the gathered priesthood of all the Christians, regularly preach the gospel and administer the ordinances. Nevertheless, Luther reminds us, each Christian must preach the gospel in and through his or her own vocation as spouse, parent, politician, and professional.[6]

Social Justice

While Christians recognize their responsibility to be "priests" to one another within the church, they also acknowledge the biblical injunction to be of service to the greater community. The twentieth-century Baptist leader Herschel H. Hobbs wrote that "the Christian citizen is to be in the world but not of it," and that he or she "is to change society not by violence but by influence and witness (Matt. 5:13-16)." Hobbs noted that people "are not saved by social reform (Rom. 10:3), yet the gospel has its social aspects (cf. Epistle of James; see also Matt. 5:13-14; 7:24ff; 25:31ff.)."[7]

Baptists have joined other Christians in recognizing that God has called the church to serve those around us. Jesus devoted much of his earthly ministry to healing the sick and the demon-possessed, and he

announced that he was anointed "to preach good news to the poor,
. . . to proclaim freedom for the prisoners and recovery of sight for
the blind, to release the oppressed, to proclaim the year of the Lord's
favor" (Luke 4:18-19). Baptists then join other believers in our Judeo-
Christian injunction to follow in Jesus' ways "to act justly and to love
mercy and to walk humbly with [our] God" (Micah 6:8).

Seeking to help the poor, the oppressed, and the victims of great
calamity have long been part and parcel of Baptist work. From initi-
ating disaster relief work to founding the first Baptist Sunday schools
(which were initially established to help community literacy), from
developing church food pantries, Baptist hospitals, and homes for
orphans to establishing avenues to curb racism, Baptists have been on
the forefront of serving a society in need. Lai Ling Ngan's sermon to
follow, then, devotes itself to the notion that, as disciples of Jesus, Baptists must be active in serving those around them in the Spirit of Christ.

Under its section entitled "The Christian and the Social Order,"
the 1963 *Baptist Faith and Message* encourages Baptists to

> work to provide for the orphaned, the needy, the aged, the helpless,
> and the sick. Every Christian should seek to bring industry, govern-
> ment, and society as a whole under the sway of the principles of
> righteousness, truth, and brotherly love. In order to promote these
> ends Christians should be ready to work with all [people] of good
> will in any good cause, always being careful to act in the spirit of
> love without compromising their loyalty to Christ and His truth.

Baptists then understand social justice to be an essential part of
their Christian witness and work.

Christian Mission

As ministers, all Baptist Christians also come to see their role as missionaries and their local church as a missional institution. While such
terminology may be new to the Baptist tradition, Baptists were pioneers of the modern missionary movement among Protestants, sending specially called missionaries around the world to share the good
news of Christ Jesus. At the same time, Baptists have understood each
member as playing a role in missions.

English Particular Baptists Andrew Fuller and William Carey were instrumental leaders in transitioning the Baptist tradition to consider evangelism and its cause for world missions at the turn of the eighteenth century. While Fuller moderated the heretofore Hyper-Calvinism of the Particular Baptists, Carey helped shape the first Baptist missionary-sending agency and served as one of its first missionaries.[8] Their understanding of the Great Commission (Matthew 28:18-20) as applicable not only to the eleven disciples remaining with the resurrected Christ but also to Christians of their day became a significant shift in focus and brought a greater consciousness to unreached peoples across the globe. Ever since this eventful development, Baptists have sent missionaries to the "four corners" of the world. However, Baptists have come to see their own churches and even themselves as missionaries in the places they live and work. Likewise, as the gathered priesthood, Baptist Christians see the church as basic to God's missionary design. Norman Maring and Winthrop Hudson observe that if the church "becomes so preoccupied with analyzing its own nature and conducting its internal affairs that it forgets its mission to the world, it ceases to be the church."[9] Thus, as Amy Jacober outlines in her sermon to follow, Baptists understand Christian mission to be integral to their responsibilities in following Christ. Baptist congregations have voluntarily joined with one another in various organizational, associational, and denominational entities for the purpose of supporting missionaries both abroad and domestically. But many Baptist congregations have also apprehended this Christian duty as encompassing the work of the local church for the purposes of evangelism and social justice in the neighborhoods and region in which each congregation ministers.

Finally, Baptists perceive the missionary call to be given by God not just to those who dedicate themselves to this vocation around the world, but to each and every individual, carrying out a role as a Christian missionary in daily tasks as a member of the priesthood of all believers. Thus, E. Y. Mullins concludes, "The duty of every Christian and the duty of every church of Christ is to seek to extend the gospel to the ends of the earth. No Christian and no church is exempt from this obligation."[10]

Notes

1. H. Leon McBeth, "God Gives Soul Competency and Priesthood to All Believers," in *Defining Baptist Convictions: Guidelines for the Twenty-First Century*, ed. Charles W. Deweese (Franklin, TN: Providence House, 1996), 63.
2. W. R. White, *Baptist Distinctives* (Nashville: Sunday School Board of the Southern Baptist Convention, 1946), 25.
3. James Leo Garrett, *Baptist Theology: A Four-Century Study* (Macon, GA: Mercer University Press, 2009), 8.
4. Robert G. Torbet, *The Baptist Ministry: Then and Now* (Philadelphia: Judson Press, 1953), 9.
5. Nigel G. Wright, *Free Church, Free State: The Positive Baptist Vision* (Milton Keynes: Paternoster, 2005), 160.
6. See Brian C. Brewer, "'These Are the Masks of God': Martin Luther and the Protestant Life of Vocation," in *Thriving in Babylon: Essays in Honor of A. J. Conyers*, ed. David B. Capes and J. Daryl Charles, Princeton Theological Monograph Series (Eugene, OR: Pickwick Publications, 2010), 178–203.
7. Herschel H. Hobbs, *What Baptists Believe* (Nashville: B&H Books, 1964), 121.
8. On October 2, 1792, a group of fourteen members of the Northampton Association in England met in the home of the widow Martha Wallace in Kettering to form the Particular Baptist Society for the Propagation of the Gospel among the Heathen, which became known more popularly as the Baptist Missionary Society. See H. Leon McBeth, *The Baptist Heritage: Four Centuries of Baptist Witness* (Nashville: B&H Academics, 1987), 185–87.
9. Norman H. Maring and Winthrop S. Hudson, *A Baptist Manual of Polity and Practice*, rev. ed. (Valley Forge, PA: Judson Press, 1991), 30.
10. E. Y. Mullins, *Baptist Beliefs* (Valley Forge, PA: Judson Press, 1925), 73.

Action Steps for the Reader

1. For further reading on Christian responsibility:

Guder, Darrell L., ed. *Missional Church: A Vision for the Sending of the Church in North America*. Grand Rapids: Eerdmans, 1998.

Luther, Martin. *The Freedom of a Christian*. Trans. Mark D. Tranvik. Minneapolis: Fortress, 2008.

Rauschenbusch, Walter. *A Theology for the Social Gospel.* 1917.

Shurden, Walter B., ed. *The Priesthood of All Believers. Proclaiming the Baptist Vision* 1. Macon, GA: Smyth & Helwys, 1993.

2. Biblical texts for preaching and topical Bible study:

Soul competency: Matthew 10:28; 22:21; 23:10; John 4:23-24; Acts 5:29; Romans 13:1-7; 14:4.

The priesthood of all believers: Exodus 19:6; 29; Ephesians 4:11-12,15-16; Hebrews 10:19-22; 1 Peter 2:9-10.

Social justice: Deuteronomy 15:7-11; Leviticus 19:9-10; Micah 6:6-8; Zechariah 7:8-10; Matthew 5:42; 25:31-46.

Christian mission: Matthew 28:18-20; Mark 16:15-17; Luke 24:47-49; Acts 1:6-8.

3. Ideas for worship:

Create a service in which worshipers are invited to pass through a veil to enter symbolically into the presence of God, individually but in the company of the saints.

Observe the Lord's Supper one Lord's Day by emphasizing that in the passing of the trays each member serves the elements to the next member. This idea underscores Carlyle Marney's concept of "priests at my elbows" in Joel Gregory's sermon.

Highlight a month with missions emphasis in your church whereby flags of various nations are brought into the sanctuary representing each country where there are missionaries supported by your own congregation. Include also your own national and state flags to emphasize work done at home as well as abroad. Then preach a series on the call to missions to the unreached and underprivileged across the world and within the vicinity of your church.

Have a special footwashing service, whether with your entire congregation, diaconate, or Sunday school class, where the leaders wash the feet (or hands) of the other members, representing Christ's servant leadership and an egalitarian priesthood.

4. Opportunities for service:

Create "priestly" and missional opportunities for the members of your congregation by serving meals at a local soup kitchen, working on a Habitat for Humanity building project, and organizing a short trip to an underprivileged part of your city or state where prayer and service are the focus.

Organize a prayer ministry in your church in which volunteers gather to pray for the concerns of the members of your congregation. Send each member who is prayed for a postcard letting him or her know the church's concern and expressing encouragement through its prayers.

CHAPTER 3

A SERMON ON THE BAPTIST DISTINCTIVE OF
Soul Competency

Conforming to Christ's Spirit, Not to the Crowd

DAVID E. GARLAND

Galatians 2:1-10

"Soul competency" refers to the God-given freedom and ability of persons to know and respond to God's will. It assumes that God allows human beings to make choices, and that they are held accountable for their choices.

I am not sure that I had any choice to be a Baptist. I was raised in a Baptist pastor's home. "Baptistness" is in my DNA. However, I believe in soul competency not because I am a Baptist and this is what Baptists believe, but because it is scriptural. I am not impressed with scriptural proof texts normally cited to support a doctrine. In my view, they tend to be rather banal and platitudinous. What captures my attention is how a doctrine reveals itself to be true in the living out the Christian faith in community—how it works itself out in practice, particularly when it is evident in the life of the early Christians. That is why I want to look at the case study of Paul and the crisis in the Galatian churches to show that soul competency is at the core of biblical theology.

Intruders had meddled with the churches Paul founded in Galatia and subverted the gospel that he preached. In the process, they also sought to undermine Paul's influence. Reading between the lines of the letter, we can guess what they may have said to sabotage him and his gospel. They attacked his authority as an apostle by claiming that he was not on the level of the pillar apostles, the original disciples of Jesus. This attack explains why Paul so vigorously defends his apostolic calling in Galatians 1:1,11-12. He is not circling the wagons to protect his wounded pride. His primary concern is not his personal reputation as an apostle, but rather the preservation of the truth of the gospel as revealed to him by Christ. That good news specifically relates to the inclusion of the Gentiles on the basis of faith and not works of law (Galatians 2:6). His particular understanding of the good news is closely tied to his apostolic self-consciousness because that was what was revealed to him when he was called to be an apostle. If someone attacks his apostleship, his gospel is attacked; if someone attacks his gospel, his apostleship is attacked.

The opponents may also have accused Paul of being a crowd-pleaser (Galatians 1:10), playing to the audience to win applause and trimming the gospel to fit what the people want to hear. Paul's gospel, they claim, has lost its cutting edge; he omitted a number of essential requirements, such as circumcision, to get a better response. As a result, they argue, Paul's gospel is defective (Galatians 3:3). He claims that all one needs to do to attain salvation is place trust in Christ. That is fine as far as it goes, his opponents maintain, but it does not go far enough. These Judaizers argue that a person can be a child of Abraham and an heir to the promises (Galatians 3:29) only by accepting circumcision and living under the law.

These troublers were not malicious heretics. They were sincere and zealous men who wanted only to correct the dangerous, liberal theology of Paul. They feared that if the Galatian Gentiles listened to Paul's gospel, they would die in their sin (see Acts 15:1). One can imagine, in modern paraphrase, the sermon that they may have preached to the Galatians:

> Brother Paul has done some good pioneer work as a lieutenant of the pillar apostles. But after visiting some of his churches, we have found a common problem: theological confusion and continuing immorality [see Galatians 5:13].
>
> You know who serves in Jerusalem, the apostle Peter, the rock of the church; the apostle John, the beloved disciple; and pastor James, the brother of our blessed Savior. Paul, as you know, never saw

Jesus. He is a Johnny-come-lately, and it is understandable how he could get things confused. He has no comparable authority like the pillar apostles [Galatians 2:9], who received their commission directly from Jesus.

Paul did not tell you the full gospel, only a condensed version. You know how he is a hit-and-run preacher, and he does not take time to give you in-depth discipleship training. Maybe he was afraid that the whole gospel was too hard for you, so he omitted some key points. But, alas, the immorality among you shows you what happens.

So, open up your Bibles to Genesis 17:9-14, and let us share with you from God's word what God commands about circumcision. Look what Abraham, the first proselyte, did. If you want to be a true child of Abraham like Isaac, you must be circumcised. Do you want to side with us, who represent the founding apostles in Jerusalem, or do you want to be left out in the cold, like Hagar and Ishmael, excluded from the people of God?

We can see how Paul was backed into a corner. His opponents had gathered a ready following because they offered a prescription for the Galatians' moral problems: the reason they are having problems is that they are still outside of the law and God's covenant. They also offered concrete religious rites to insure their salvation. A rite of obedience must have offered a greater sense of security to the Galatians than just believing in an invisible Christ. They could now point to something that they had done for salvation. The opponents could also cite Scripture. The Bible says, "You must be circumcised, or else!"

Paul's response to this defamation of his gospel in our text, Galatians 2:1-10, reveals the heart of the matter and shows soul competency at work. Paul has been engaged in his mission preaching for over fourteen years. He has not been back to Jerusalem except for a two-week stint and did not receive his apostolic commission or his gospel from the apostles there. But he did go back to Jerusalem to meet with the pillar apostles because of "a revelation" (2:1-2). This passage is the only place in Paul's letters that he says he did something on the basis of a revelation. He does not expand on it by saying to whom the revelation was made. Did it come to him personally, to a Christian prophet, or to the church? He does not say. It is unimportant. What is important is this: by saying that he went according to a revelation, he makes clear (1) that he was not summoned by those in Jerusalem; (2) that he did not go there because of any personal motivation, because of any theological insecurity, doubt, or difficulties on his part; (3) that it was God's will and not his or anyone else's; he simply obeyed a divine command.

He then says, "Then I laid before them (though only in a private meeting with the acknowledged leaders) the gospel that I proclaim among the Gentiles, in order to make sure that I was not running, or had not run, in vain" (2:2). At first reading, this statement might suggest that Paul was concerned that he could be wrong in his views, so he presented his gospel to the experts in Jerusalem for their inspection so that they might discern and correct any errors. *The Jerusalem Bible* reflects this kind of thinking in its translation: "I did so for fear the course I was adopting would not be allowed." *The New Testament in Modern English* paraphrases, "To make sure that what I had done and proposed doing was acceptable to them." These renderings could give the false impression that Paul feared that the Jerusalem leaders would give him an "F" in mission theology and practice.

He was not afraid, however, that they might say to him, "You are missing a basic component of the gospel." Nor was he seeking reassurance from them that he was on the right track. He has already told the Galatians, "For I want you to know, brothers and sisters, that the gospel that was proclaimed by me is not of human origin; for I did not receive it from a human source, nor was I taught it, but I received it through a revelation of Jesus Christ" (1:11-12). Paul was not worried about the truth of the gospel he preached. He was concerned about the effect that the decisions of influential members of the Jerusalem church might have on his converts, who believed that gospel. *The New Jerusalem Bible* corrects the previous translation, reading, "to make quite sure that the efforts I was making and had already made should not be fruitless."

The disapproval of his work and his theology by leading apostles in Jerusalem would precipitate an irreparable rupture in the church. The church would break up into Jewish Christian and Gentile Christian factions that would seriously harm the mission to the Gentiles.

How do you preach a gospel of reconciliation leaving behind an unreconciled church? How do you preach God's acceptance of sinners when Jewish Christians find Gentile Christians unacceptable? Paul engages in theological warfare with opponents because he is concerned about the theological welfare of his converts, both past and future. If he does not convince the leaders in Jerusalem about his gospel, then his converts may be lured away by a false gospel.

Therefore, Paul went to Jerusalem ostensibly to consult with the leaders there, but really to challenge and convince them. He intended to have a showdown. He did not go as a defendant, like a young Martin Luther having to answer charges before the Holy Roman emperor Charles V at the Diet of Worms. He went as a plaintiff. Why else take Titus along? The presence of Titus was intentionally provocative. It was like bringing a black to a white church in the dark days of segregation, when some churches shut doors to anyone of color even with the sign out front that said, "God loves you! We do too! You all come!"

I remember when we had some Africans staying in our home, and my parents deliberately took them to an association mission meeting that was being held at a church in the area that was known for excluding blacks. Here are persons who were converted through Baptist missions. Will you lock arms and bar them from entering your church?

Taking the uncircumcised Titus along, then, was deliberately provocative. What would the apostles do when confronted by the evidence of an uncircumcised Gentile convert such as Titus? It was difficult for many Jewish Christians, who had been indoctrinated from childhood to believe that circumcision was the seal of the covenant, to think that circumcision was now something of no importance. How would Gentiles suddenly become acceptable to God without becoming circumcised? The false teachers say, "If you are not circumcised, you cannot be saved" (cf. Acts 15:1). Paul says, "If you do get circumcised to become saved, you cut yourself off from Christ" (see Galatians 5:2-4). There can be no compromise.

Nothing happened to Titus in Jerusalem, but it was not for want of trying by the diehard hardliners. Paul uses unflattering terms to describe them. In Galatians 2:4 they are, literally, "false brothers" (*pseudadelphoi*). But this could refer to someone who is not a brother at all. Since "brother" is synonymous with "Christian," it could mean that they were "insidious impostors." In 2 Corinthians 11:26 Paul lists the various dangers that he had faced: rivers, robbers, his own people, Gentiles (pagans), in the city, in the wilderness, at sea, and, danger from "false brothers" (again, *pseudadelphoi*). Paul says that false brothers had infiltrated the ranks of the Galatian believers to "spy out" their freedom. To "spy out" implies more than gathering information; it is to lie in wait for someone. Their ultimate goal is to "enslave" the believers, to put them back under the guard of the law.

The rough syntax in Galatians 2:3-5 reflects Paul's emotional turmoil in recalling the underhandedness of the opponents at Jerusalem. Martin Luther wrote, "Anyone who is inflamed while speaking cannot at the same time observe grammatical rules." I have taught in that situation where students were encouraged to tape record professors secretly to catch them in so-called heresy, where students deliberately asked loaded questions to trap professors, where students befriended professors to snag them in some theological indiscretion, where students scoured professors' writings to find hints of heresy, no matter if it was taken out of context. And there was a central clearinghouse that collected all the gathered information and kept track to reward loyal students with promises of future advancement. These are bitter memories, and although I think that I have managed to observe grammatical rules in recounting them, I do understand something of Paul's anger.

Paul presented his gospel to those who were "reputed to be something" (2:6, RSV). The meaning "reputed" is unique in Paul's usage of this Greek verb (*dokeō*). He probably did not come up with this designation of the Jerusalem leaders on his own; rather, he picks up a phrase used by others, perhaps his opponents, to refer reverently to them. They were those of repute, the pillars, the notables, the bigwigs, the luminaries, and the titular heads of the church. But Paul says that what they are makes no difference as far as God or the truth of the gospel is concerned.

"What they once were" probably is to be taken in a positive vein, but it could also have a negative connotation. They had abandoned

Jesus at the moment of crisis and, in Peter's case, denied him. None of these advantages or deficiencies is important to God. That is why Paul says, "They contributed nothing to me." It does not mean that he got little out of hearing them. The "me" refers to Paul's gospel that he preached and shows how the two were so closely tied together in his mind: he was called by God to preach a certain gospel. It means that they added no restrictions or further requirements to the proclamation of his gospel. There were to be no asterisks, no fine print: "The Gospel Is Absolutely Free*" (*Circumcision required in most cases).

The Greek word *tounantion* in 2:7 draws a contrast between the Jerusalem leaders and the false brethren: not only did the leaders add no new restraints, but also, on the contrary (*tounantion*), they gave Paul an unqualified endorsement. They publicly acknowledged that God's action that made Peter an apostle also made Paul an apostle. They recognized that God, who worked through Peter as his apostle among the Jews, also worked through Paul among the Gentiles.

The reaction of James, Cephas, and John to the gospel that Paul laid before them dominates his account of his visit. One can easily see why. These pillars of the church recognized the validity of Paul's gospel and his apostleship. They discerned the grace given to Paul and confirmed the legitimacy of his preaching and his mission among the Gentiles. But—and everything leads to this point—Paul's report is ambivalent. On the one hand, Paul concedes their authority. They were apostles before he was (Galatians 1:18). Cephas (Peter) and John were followers of Jesus, called by Jesus himself from their fishing nets, and James was the brother of Jesus. They could pass on traditions about the earthly Jesus that no one else could (Galatians 1:18-19). They are of repute; they are the pillar apostles. And they confirmed that God was working through Paul. They extended to him the right hand of fellowship and agreed that he should proceed unhindered with his ministry to the uncircumcised. In other words, they did not challenge the truth of the gospel that he preached; they certified it. That they did not compel Titus to be circumcised proves that they ratified his gospel. They gave him the theological equivalent of the Good Housekeeping Seal of approval.

However, Paul strongly maintains that even though they were pillar apostles, whatever they were meant nothing to him and nothing to God (Galatians 2:6). God does not care about their reputations, and neither does he (see 2 Corinthians 5:12). Paul was not awed by them, by their history, by their lofty status. Why, then, does he show such ambivalence toward these apostles? It does not derive from some rivalry with them. His reservations are centered on the main issue in this section and the entire epistle: the truth of the gospel (Galatians 2:5,14), and that it might abide for the Gentiles.

Paul has made it clear that he was dependent on no one except Jesus for his gospel (Galatians 1:17-18), and that the pillar apostles added nothing to it (Galatians 2:6). He knows that the truth of the gospel does not depend on the certification of any human. He did not get an apostle certificate from them. He did not get letters of recommendation from them. He did not get a *nihil obstat* from them to place on his letters to certify that they are free from doctrinal or moral error. He did not get an *imprimatur* from them. The gospel is not "according to humans" (*kata anthrōpon*) (Galatians 1:11). One cannot depend on external, human criteria to determine what the truth of the gospel is.

Paul wants to set the record straight for the deceived Galatians. The apostles that they have heard so much about did happen to ratify his gospel. They ratified his authority as an apostle. They ratified his work among the uncircumcised. But their ratification makes no difference as far as the truth of the gospel is concerned or his authority as an apostle. If they had not recognized the truth of the gospel, they would not have been true apostles, regardless of their pedigree, regardless of their office, regardless of their stature, regardless of their reputation. As a matter of fact, there was some slippage on the part of Peter and others in Antioch (Galatians 2:11-14). They turned away from the truth of the gospel by refusing to eat with Gentile Christians, and Paul confronted Peter and everyone, including Barnabas, face to face.

Paul's underlying assumption is that the truth of the gospel does not depend on any human certification no matter how revered that human or group of humans might be. The pillar authorities gave their stamp of approval to his gospel, but that approval does not make his gospel true. They are not the final court of appeal. Their recognition of the truth of the gospel says more about the character of the apostles and their God-given ability to perceive God's truth than it says about Paul's gospel. They upheld the truth of the gospel, but its truth does not depend on their approval. It does not depend on public opinion polls, on those with the highfalutin academic degrees, on imposing church councils, on carefully crafted church creeds, or on the votes of church leaders.

Their authority, anyone's authority in the church, depends entirely on whether they uphold the truth of the gospel. It means that no one, no pope, no college of cardinals, no bishops, no denomination, no association of churches can dictate to anyone what the truth of the gospel is.

The emphasis is on "dictate." In the early 1980s, while the controversy in the Southern Baptist Convention was in its early stages, several pastors were invited to meet in Atlanta to discuss the differences that divided and threatened to destroy the convention. It was called the "peace committee." There was dialogue concerning the importance of academic freedom in the educational processes of seminaries and colleges. A leader of the takeover movement said at the meeting, "Southern Baptist seminary professors must teach whatever they are told to teach. And if we [the Southern Baptist Convention] tell them to teach that pickles have souls, then they must teach that pickles have souls!" Those were his exact words.

What would Paul have done had the Jerusalem leaders refused to accept his gospel? What would Paul have done had they insisted that he alter his gospel to require circumcision? Would he have returned to Antioch and told the Gentiles, "Well, we gave it our best shot, but they outvoted us. We will have to give in"? Paul never would have obeyed human dictates and disobeyed what he knew God had called him to do (see 1 Corinthians 9:8). He would have continued doing the same thing he had been doing, but with a sad heart, realizing that important leaders failed to see the whole truth of the gospel, and that Christ, the church, was divided.

But how do you know the truth of the gospel? Soul competency does not mean that sole competency belongs to you. The truth of the gospel is discerned in community, as it was for Paul. He was not a maverick. One should be careful before thinking "I alone am being faithful" and whining like Elijah: "I have been very zealous for the

LORD, the God of hosts; for the Israelites have forsaken your covenant, thrown down your altars, and killed your prophets with the sword. I alone am left" (1 Kings 19:10,14). God says, "Yet I will leave seven thousand in Israel, all the knees that have not bowed to Baal" (1 Kings 19:18). Each one of us knows the truth of the gospel and the grace of God only in using us for, and receiving from us, from others.

CHAPTER 4

A SERMON ON THE BAPTIST DISTINCTIVE OF THE
Priesthood of All Believers

Impersonating a Priest

JOEL C. GREGORY

Matthew 27:51

H e was a familiar face around the Our Lady of Mt. Carmel Church
on East 187th Street in the Bronx section of New York. On warm
Sunday afternoons he would sit outside the church and counsel the
young people from the predominantly Italian neighborhood around
that church. He seemed to speak with the erudition that ought to char-
acterize a Jesuit priest who taught canon law at Fordham University.
Also, he had an air of endless compassion about him.

He was there so often that the priest of the church invited him to
celebrate Mass. They were somewhat surprised when he stumbled
through it, especially since he claimed to be a Jesuit. And once, in the
chapel, he actually baptized a baby of some members in the parish,
although they wondered why he never gave them a baptismal certificate. Finally, on a July day the New York City police caught up with
him. He was not really Father Giuseppe Visconti, as he claimed to be;
his real name was "John Fortune." He was thirty-five years old and
had no formal training as a priest. He was arrested for impersonating a priest. Indeed, he had conducted five Masses, heard numerous
confessions, and even baptized one baby. The story brings to mind
Frank Abagnale, the character played by Leonardo DiCaprio in the
movie, *Catch Me If You Can*.

Yet we are not under any danger of *impersonating* a priest. One
of the Baptist distinctives declares that if you are a believer, you are

indeed a priest. It is not so much a doctrine among doctrines as it is a way of looking at every other Christian teaching. It is a vantage point from which we look, a tinted lens through which we view the rest of the Christian life—and life together, for that matter. The priesthood of believers is not just one room in the Baptist house; it is the very atmosphere that pervades every room in that house. It is a way of being as a Baptist believer. Because God says that you are a priest, it is a way of living out your experience in the faith. In short, the priesthood of believers is the way you see yourself because it is the way God sees you.

Matthew 27:51 is just one verse in a passage that describes those striking events that were wordless affirmations of what happened at Calvary. It was around the time of the evening sacrifice that Friday at Herod's temple, the third and last iteration of that institution in Jerusalem. Because it was a busy day at the temple, there were many sons of Aaron there efficiently pushing the buttons and pulling the levers of the sanctuary. The pungent odor of the incense filled their flared nostrils. By that time, their hands were probably caked with the blood and gore of running the mechanics of the institution. If you listened, you could almost hear the clip-clop of their sandaled feet against the hard Herodian stones. Maybe they were walking around with the kind of officiousness that belongs to little people in a very big place, just like that U.S. Supreme Court police officer who recently ran a friend of mine off the front steps of that building. In effect, the officer was saying, "How dare you sit in front of the building given to the interpretation of the Constitution that says you could sit there!"

Those priests may have thought that they had the institution; in reality, however, the institution had them. But it had not always been that way. When God imparted the concept of the priesthood to Moses in Exodus 4, he was essentially saying, "I'm going to speak to you, and then you'll speak to Aaron, and Aaron will speak to the people." According to British scholar Cyril Eastwood, the priesthood was first established with a didactic function. The priests were set apart to be teachers of the will and the way of Yahweh. But something happened during those forty years between Exodus 4 and Moses' farewell message near his 120th birthday, recorded in Deuteronomy 33. It would have been as if Steve Jobs came back to

Apple to remind his employees about the company's mission statement. Addressing the Levites, Moses said, "No, you've got it wrong.
It is God's intention that you keep his word, teach his ordinances,
interpret his will, and lead his worship." Perhaps even Moses began
to sense that instead of standing alongside the people and coming
from among them, the priests were beginning to stand over them.

For what began as a didactic function gradually became sacerdotal, and what became sacerdotal became a kind of mediatorship
between the people and Yahweh. By the time Micah wrote his third
chapter to rebuke the priests of Israel, the temple gig had become a
good way to make a buck. Basically, the priests were telling the people, "You pay me, and I will 'priest' you."

Back again in Matthew 27, Joe the priest, a member of the priesthood from the cohorts that came up to the temple from time to time,
was standing there that Good Friday afternoon. He had come from
a little town such as Nain, Cana, or Tiberius. Who knows how Joe
felt at the time. Perhaps he was standing there in awe. Perhaps he was
frightened that he would drop some implement, like the Baptist deacon frightened of dropping a plate at the Lord's Supper service. Perhaps Joe was bored with the same kind of boredom that comes from
hanging around temples. (This happens even around seminaries,
where you handle holy things all the time.) Perhaps he was just hungry and wanted to get off work and go for a corned beef sandwich.
Perhaps he was wondering whether the kickoff was at noon or three.
At any rate, Joe was there.

It had been an ordinary day at the temple except for one thing:
an unscheduled eclipse. For some time in the midst of the day, it
became midnight at midday; yet the priests went ahead and did their
work, their shadows dancing in the light of the menorah that lit the
Holy Place.

Joe found himself standing before a national monument, like our
Lincoln Memorial: the temple veil. The writings of Josephus and the
Talmud report that this veil was sixty feet wide, thirty feet tall, and
as thick as a person's hand. They record that it took as many as three
hundred priests to manipulate the enormous drapery on its giant curtain rod. This veil featured embroideries and fabrics that resembled

the zodiac wheel—the color blue representing the sky, crimson the sun, and flaxen the earth. Once a year, one person went behind the veil: the high priest.

But then, in the midst of all of the sameness, the extraordinary happened. The Synoptic Gospels record, "The curtain of the temple was torn in two." Literally, there was a schism in the drapery. The passive voice is used—the passive voice of divine action. In other words, it was God who had split it from the inaccessible top to bottom. The unseen finger of the unseen actor tore the veil. In order to make sure that we understand, the verse emphasizes that the veil hung in two, completely torn asunder. Later Jewish tradition caught a garbled significance of this. One of the stories recounted that, at about this time, the temple doors had swung open by themselves. Another version mentioned that the menorah in the Holy Place had gone out. Matthew reminds us with a series of staccato aorist verbs that the earth was shaken, the rocks were split, and the tombs were opened.

For Joe the priest, it was the equivalent of standing in front of the Jefferson Memorial while the giant statue of Jefferson toppled over or beneath Mount Rushmore while a presidential face or two fell off. It was the most unimaginable thing that could have happened. Joe suddenly looks at what he could not, would not, and must not look at—the very Holy of Holies, the most holy of places. To look was to die, and to touch was sheer suicide.

What did Joe the priest do next? Perhaps he sent a text message to Caiaphas the high priest that said, "Get the temple guild together. Bring everyone who has needles and thread. We've got to sew this thing up before anyone knows what has happened." (Institutions do what it takes to keep going. The people running them are experts at survival; that is why they are called "institutions.")

On that day, at that moment, with the eyes of the heart, you could have looked into the sky and seen an angel writing this message in the clouds over the temple in Jerusalem: "Out of Business." With the right eyes, you could have seen a mighty seraph descending to place this real estate sign in front of the temple's golden gates: "Relocated. See Pentecost.com for more information." With the right ears, Joe the priest could have heard this message spoken to him by a cherub:

"You'd better get down to the Jerusalem Workforce Commission and apply for unemployment, because you're out of a job. As of now, any believer in Jesus can have your job."

Nobody knew it yet, but it was that time. The rending of the veil is a screaming symbol of what we hold precious as Baptist believers. The sacred writers exult in this reality: the pros no longer control the game. In fact, you could drop Hebrews 8 right down into the gap between those torn curtains. Here is a better, greater high priest who has gone into a greater, better tabernacle with a greater, better sacrifice—his own blood—not annually, but one time so that God might write his ordinance on the warm, quivering flesh of our new hearts. You could also insert 1 Peter 2:9 right into the gap in that torn curtain: "You are a chosen race, a royal priesthood, a holy nation, God's own people." Toward the end of the century on the island of Patmos, the apostle John wrote at the beginning of the apocalyptic book of Revelation that Jesus Christ has made us to be "priests serving his God and Father" (Revelation 1:6). Before he put his pen down, John wrote of faithful believers as "priests of God and of Christ" (Revelation 20:6).

The German Reformer Martin Luther put it this way: "Everyone who has been baptized may claim that he has been consecrated bishop, priest, or pope." Timothy George, dean and professor at Beeson Divinity School, wrote, "The distinct contribution of the Reformers to ecclesiology is the priesthood of the believer." In his own unique way, French Reformer John Calvin wrote it while affirming the uniqueness of the priesthood of Christ: "There is no priest but Christ, yet it is the duty of every Christian to offer spiritual sacrifices as a priest in solidarity with the priesthood of Christ." The Swiss Reformer Ulrich Zwingli affirmed, "It is true that we are fully ordained to the priesthood." Four hundred years ago, John Smyth, that other John the Baptist, wrote, "We have all power, both of the kingdom and the priesthood, immediately from Christ." The twentieth-century British Baptist scholar H. Wheeler Robinson wrote, "Not only can we claim the priesthood of the believer, but we can claim the prophethood of the believer, for the task of evangelism and missions belong to all of us."

Everywhere you find those who have written about the Baptist heritage—Broadus, Truett, Shurden, Hobbs, Estep, McBeth—these great apologists for the Baptist faith say, "This is the way we look at the Christian life: through the lens of being believer-priests." What does that mean? It means that because of this rent veil, we as Christian believers share both the privilege of access and the burden of responsibility.

First, we have the privilege of access—access in the matter of our own salvation. When it comes to salvation, we have one mediator, our Lord Jesus Christ. We stand there between law and grace, trouble and help. If we do not understand that this is, in a sense, a terror-filled place as well as a grace-filled place to stand, then we do not understand the narrow edge that it is. The apostle Paul said in Philippians 2:12, "Work out your own salvation with fear and trembling," because there is nobody else there besides your Savior and you when it comes to salvation. You will not be able to point to Rome, Canterbury, or Nashville or look to the pope, a cardinal, a bishop, or even your local pastor. Like Joe the priest, you will stand there, peering through that curtain alone.

Indeed, T. M. Lindsay eloquently writes, "The one principle of the Reformation is *the priesthood of all believers*—the right of every believing man and woman, whether lay or cleric, to go to God directly with confession seeking pardon, with ignorance seeking enlightenment, with solitary loneliness seeking fellowship, with frailty and weakness seeking strength for daily holy living."[1] The veil is torn.

Inside that rent veil is the personal priesthood of confession and absolution. When I get inside that veil, I am looking for mediation in my confession only through the Lord Jesus Christ—no hierarchy, no cabal made up of anyone else. Inside that veil with the aimlessness of my own sinning, the rebellion of my own transgression, and the twisted nature of my own iniquity, I confess like David and say, "Against you, you alone, have I sinned" (Psalm 51:4).

But that is where we sometimes miss something in this doctrine: all of us have the keys. Calvin cites both Cyprian and Augustine in noting that the gift of the keys was made not to Peter only; the gift was given to everyone that day, including us. Jesus said that what we bind is bound, and what we loose is loosed (Matthew 16:19). In the words of Carlyle Marney, we are priests to one another. I do not listen for the phrase *ego te absolvo* (I absolve you) to come from any human being. I can confess to you, and you can confess to me, and we can be priests at each other's elbow. John Claypool observed that Baptists have been a whole lot better at making guilt an event than they have at making forgiveness an event. It is our place as believer-priests to make forgiveness an event for one another.

Inside that rent veil, you also gain bold access in prayer through the person of the Lord Jesus Christ. Again, you can drop a Scripture down into the gap in that shredded curtain, Hebrews 10:19-22: "Therefore, my friends, since we have confidence to enter the sanctuary by the blood of Jesus, by the new and living way that he opened for us, through the curtain (that is, through his flesh), and since we have a great priest over the house of God, let us approach with a true heart in full assurance of faith."

One day during the presidency of Abraham Lincoln, a group of backwoodsmen were milling around the White House grounds, complaining that they could not get in to see Old Abe. For political reasons, Lincoln did not wish to see them. But his son Robert heard them. He took the leader by the hand and led these people, who had no access, straight into the office of his father. Likewise, Jesus, God's Son, has provided the way for us to have an audience with the heavenly Father.

Inside that rent veil, we also gain access to Scripture. In short, the Bible becomes an open book to us because of what Jesus has done. It is part of our priceless heritage to have direct access to this book, not through a magisterium. We may acknowledge the creeds. We may be able to cite Constantinople, Nicea, Chalcedon, and the rest, but they do not put a veil over this book. Nor does any order of scholars, professors, exegetes, or theologians do so. It is not that everyone is equally able to interpret this book—God, keep us from that—but everyone can find sufficient material in the Bible for all that is needed for personal faith and its practice.

As a reminder of this fact, I keep four Bibles in a glass case in my study. The oldest one belonged to my great-grandfather, Calvin Gregory, who was a Texas Baptist farmer and preacher in 1850, when Baylor University was just five years old. Sometimes I get it out and look at it. There are pencil marks in the margins that I can barely see.

This is the Bible that Texas farmer-preacher used as he took his place as a believer-priest, put down his plow, and preached to the farmers under a brush arbor in Jack County.

Beside that Bible is one given to my paternal grandfather, Albert C. Gregory, by his mother-in-law, Nancy Hornback, in 1917. He would come home at noon, a break in the day from plowing behind a mule, and read that Bible as a believer-priest. Next to that Bible is one given by my late mother, Edith, to my late father, Clifford, on Easter 1965, marked up with little notes from a men's Bible class at Connell Baptist Church in Fort Worth, Texas. By that Bible is a little one that I was given as a nine-year-old, with all my childish scrawls across it. I had written on the flyleaf, "Property of Joel Gregory. Return at once if found." It is a reminder to me from generation to generation that we are not dependent on any "reverend doctor" to come to the book and meet God there.

Inside that rent veil, however, there is not only privilege, but also the burden of responsibility. We have torqued the concept of the priesthood of the believer into an excuse for individualism so that we can act like spiritual mavericks or Lone Rangers. We have made it into a philosophy that says, "I can believe whatever I want to believe, by myself, because I'm a believer-priest." But inside that veil, one of those burdens of responsibility is that I take you seriously because you are inside that veil too.

In Exodus 19 we learn that way up in the clouds on Mount Sinai, God spoke to Moses about his vision for a kingdom of priests (plural). It would be a holy nation, not a group of isolationists or mavericks, each one living autonomously. Likewise, I take you seriously because we both are inside the veil, and as Marney said, we are priests to one another.

These words from Luther ring out in truth to us today: "A shoemaker, a smith, a farmer, each has his manual occupation and work; and yet, at the same time, all are eligible to act as priests and bishops. Every one of them in his occupation or handicraft ought to be useful to his fellows, and serve them in such a way that the various trades are all directed to the best advantage of the community, and promote the well-being of body and soul, just as the organs serve one another."[2]

I take you more seriously as a farmer, a line worker, a teacher, or a litigator because your vocation is that of a holy priest in whatever you do. This means that we view the church through a different lens because the church does not come down to us from some hierarchy. In the gathered church, we are the church together.

I notice that in the list of spiritual gifts and offices described in 1 Corinthians 12:4-11,27-30 and Ephesians 4:11 there is no gift of priesthood. There were apostles, prophets, evangelists, pastors, teachers, healers, interpreters of tongues, and more, but no gift of priesthood was listed because what belongs to everybody is not the special gift of anybody. We are all believer-priests to one another.

Thomas Long writes, "When we who preach open the sanctuary door on Sunday morning and find a congregation waiting there for us, it is easy to forget that we come *from* these people, not *to* them from the outside. We are not visitors from clergy-land, strangers from an unknown land, ambassadors from seminary-land, or even, as much as we may cherish the thought, prophets from a wilderness land. We are members of the body of Christ, commissioned to preach by the very people to whom we are about to speak."[3] That is why the church should be called a fellowship instead of a membership, and a body instead of an institution. This relates directly to the priesthood of all believers.

I had a difficult moment the other day. While driving down University Parks Drive in Waco and then turning right to go to the gym to dance my dance on the elliptical machine, I noticed where the Edgefield Baptist Church had been. There it was—a pile of stone and splinters. The building had to go because it had been empty for quite a while. But it still felt like a bulldozer ran over my heart because that was the first place I ever tried to be the pastor of people. I struggled emotionally out there that day with David Hardage, who, incidentally, preached his first sermon there. He picked up a brick, and I found part of a stone sign that was over the door—the *d*, the *g*, and the *e*.

I put pieces of lettering in the trunk of my car, taking away what I could. But to keep that bulldozer from continuing to run over my heart, I remembered that this church was not an institution; it was a body. It was where Claude Edelman, a groundskeeper at Baylor University for forty years, was the chairman of the deacons. More than anyone else in my life, he "priested" me. H. B. Elliott, a laborer who built tires out at the General Tire plant, was a holy-priest tire maker. He drove a used school bus to pick up children in south Waco and then brought them to church. J. L. Martin was a holy-priest car dealer with a lot near the McLennan County courthouse. I remembered then that they could bulldoze that church, but they could never take away those who were priests to me.

The greatest truth of that rent veil is not so much the fact that it let us in, although it did. The greatest truth is that, in a very real sense, God got out. What God told Moses in Exodus 19 finally happened.

It is said that an average chess player can think only three moves ahead, and a chess master can think thirty moves ahead. But the almighty God can think a million moves ahead, and he knew how to get where he wanted to get when that veil was rent. Not only did we get in; he got out.

This means now that the division between the sacred and the secular is no more. If you are a believing truck driver, you are a holy-priest truck driver. If you work at the chicken-processing plant, you are a holy-priest chicken plucker. If you teach in a classroom, you are a holy-priest schoolteacher.

When I think of the open veil, I also realize that in other ways we are believer-priests on a journey to get to the other side of that veil to see everything that a believer-priest has not yet seen.

The Wizard of Oz is a classic American movie. Dorothy and Toto met several archetypal figures on the way. There was the scarecrow, who needed a brain, the tin man, who needed a heart, and the lion, who needed courage. Dorothy just wanted to get home. They heard about a fabulous wizard in Oz who could grant their desires. But when they arrived in Oz and saw the wizard, they looked behind the curtain, and there was nothing but disappointment—just a little old man pulling the levers.

The priesthood of all believers has a better promise. When we finally get behind the curtain, there is the great high priest, the Lord Jesus Christ, who lets us share the priesthood with him. We need a new mind, a renewed heart, and courage. We find it all in Jesus. So what I say to you, I say to all, "Let it rip."

Notes

1. T. M. Lindsay, *The Reformation* (Edinburgh: T & T Clark, 1882), 185–86.

2. Martin Luther, "An Appeal to the Ruling Class of German Nationality as to the Amelioration of the State of Christendom, 1520," in *Martin Luther: Selections from His Writings*, ed. John Dillenberger (Anchor Books, 1962), 410.

3. Thomas G. Long, *The Witness of Preaching* (Louisville: Westminster John Knox, 1990), 11.

CHAPTER 5

A SERMON ON THE BAPTIST DISTINCTIVE OF
Social Justice

True Religion of Christian Praxis

LAI LING ELIZABETH NGAN
Amos 5:10-15,24; James 2:1-17

The books of Amos and James are my favorite books in the Bible because they speak to God's people about how to live out the gospel in practical terms. Though they were speaking to communities that existed more than two thousand years ago, the situations against which the authors spoke are eerily similar to our modern world, and their messages are relevant for our time.

The prophet Amos was sent by God from the Southern Kingdom of Judah to preach to the Israelites in the North. The middle of the eighth century BCE in Israel was a period marked by peace, prosperity, and piety, but things were not entirely what they seemed. It is like an apple that looks perfect on the outside—it's red and shiny— but the exterior hides the rot that is consuming the flesh within. The problem with the Israelites was not their religiosity, for their religious activities and fervor were beyond reproach. The problem was injustice, social and economic injustice that robbed the poor of their land and livelihoods, that led to debt-slavery without recourse for redemption, that enriched the coffers of the wealthy, and that enabled the luxurious lifestyle of the elite. Was that not wrong? Is this not wrong in any age?

The Rich and the Poor

The society that Amos prophesied against is not unlike our society where the rich grow richer while the poor grow poorer. A report by the Survey of Consumer Finances sponsored by the Federal Reserve Board showed that in 2004, the top 1 percent of families in the United States owned 34.3 percent of this country's net worth, while the combined wealth of the bottom 40 percent comprised just 0.2 percent. To put this in more concrete terms, if a community of one hundred families were to share one hundred pounds of rice, one family would receive almost 35 pounds of the allotment, while forty families would receive less than 1 ounce of rice each. The disparity between the haves and have-nots is obscene. If the trend for the last thirty years holds true, the gap between the rich and the poor is growing worse.

Let us not stop there. The 2011 U.S. Federal Poverty Level Guidelines set the poverty line at an annual income of $14,710 for a family of two, $22,350 for a family of four, and $37,630 for a family of eight. Let's take the family of four as our example: $22,350 works out to be $1,862.50 per month, or $61.23 per day. What would it be like for your family of four to live a year on a budget of $22,350? How far would $1,862.50 per month go to cover rent, utilities, work-related expenses, food, taxes, medical insurance and additional medical costs, and incidentals? Would you give up medical insurance, or forego heat and electricity? Are diapers a necessary expenditure or frivolous luxury? What would you feed your family? For dinner, $5 would buy four single hamburgers from a fast food restaurant's dollar menu, but you would not have enough money left to get even one side salad or a small order of fries.

Healthier food costs more money, so the poor have little choice but to buy cheaper yet unhealthy food. To be poor is not a chosen way of life for most folks; the disenfranchised are pushed into it and kept in it. Large grocery chains do not put stores in poor neighborhoods because they tend to be crime-ridden, with the added cost of security resulting in lower margin of profit. This leaves the poor with little to no access to fresh produce and meat, and if these were available at the corner stores, they would be more expensive and not particularly fresh.

In comparison to the $22,350 of the 2011 U.S. Federal Poverty Level Guidelines, the international poverty level established by the World Bank is low beyond comprehension. The latest available global data (2005) standardized $1.25 USD or less per person per day as the low income level, and more than one-half of the world's population is subsisting on $2.50 or less per day. Can we conceive of living on $2.50 a day? That is $75 a month, and this figure is inclusive of housing, food, medical expenses, and any other costs related to staying alive. I cannot imagine.

The causes and ramifications of poverty are many and are interrelated. Natural disasters, political unrest, unjust legislation, perverted justice, systemic exploitation, and the list goes on. Our sinful nature, our greed and selfishness, our lust for power and wealth, our callousness toward the vulnerable and the weak of society, and that list goes on as well. Images streaming through television and the Internet inform us of the horrible conditions many people are suffering around the world: the child with the enlarged head and extended belly that result from malnutrition and starvation, the emaciated mother who cannot produce milk to feed her baby, the orphans who hide underground like rats to evade the government's eradication program, which seeks to rid the embarrassment to their tourist industry. We cannot feign ignorance of conditions around the world. The question is whether we *want* to know or not. If we reap benefits from the labor and exploitation of the poor, we are responsible for the injustice foisted on them; we are culpable.

Men and Women

Women, unfortunately, are the poorest of the poor. In sub-Saharan Africa, rural China, and many parts of South and Southeast Asia, men have to leave their families for the cities in hopes of finding work, while the women are left with caring and providing for the children and the elderly parents using traditional, nontechnical ways to produce food and collect water. They are vulnerable to drought, crop diseases, and insect invasions that can lead to famine and starvation. When political unrest breaks out, women suffer the brunt of violence from advancing bands of soldiers and rebels. The raping and killing of women is intended to emasculate the males of a community, but it is also crime against all humanity (Amos 1:13).

Such atrocities were only recognized as war crime by the United Nations in 1992, but God recognized it and Amos preached against it more than 2,700 years ago. Many charity organizations and global entities have highlighted the importance of raising the status of women and empowering them with education and financial opportunities as crucial to the eradication of poverty. Examples of projects spawned from the United Nation's Millennium Development Goals showed that providing education and microbusiness loans to poor women in India and parts of Africa has raised the living standard for their families and sometimes for their entire community, moving them from the edge of starvation to the firmer ground of a sustainable living.

Women in the United States fare far better than the poor women in developing countries, but in comparison with American males, even U.S. women remain at a disadvantage. Women from every racial-ethnic group, including whites, have a higher rate of poverty than that of men. The U.S. Census Bureau's 2009 supplemental report indicates that women's incomes continue to lag behind those of men's. Women receive 77 cents on the dollar for doing the same jobs, with the same qualifications, and working the same number of hours or more. The inequity is gendered-based. Furthermore, women often provide unpaid custodial care for children and the elderly, which is not considered work by society and the government. Women are often put into job categories that receive the lowest pay, such as cashiers at retail stores, servers in restaurants, and processers at food-canning factories. No sound moral reason can be given to sustain such an unjust system, especially if we claim to be Christians, the people of God. Can we rightly claim that half of the kingdom of God is second-class citizens?

Impoverished Opportunities

The poor of this country tend to have fewer educational opportunities and substandard quality schooling; this leads to limited career choices that make them the working-poor, that is, if they can get a job at all. They are forced to live in crime-infested neighborhoods because that is where the housing projects are located. Just cross to the other side of the freeway or the railroad tracks at the edge of town. The poor are there, but they are largely invisible to the rest of us. Have you ever tried to integrate low-income housing into a middle- or upper-middle-class neighborhood? It will not happen because money speaks. The poor, on the other hand, have neither power nor voice. How often do elected officials side with those who lack the money, power, and votes that politicians covet? This may be the American social reality, but it surely cannot be the Christian way. The legal and bureaucratic machination penalizes the poor and makes it incredibly difficult, if not outright impossible, for people in poverty to move up the social ladder and gain a better living standard.

A Biblical Mandate to Right Wrongs

The social and economic injustices in this generation are systemic and legal, similar to that in Amos's days. Throughout human history, the rich and powerful elite have established laws for their own benefit. They have levied fines on the poor, confiscated their lands, and sold them into debt-slavery. Amos proclaimed that God was about to punish the elite

> . . . because they sell the righteous for silver, and the needy for a pair of sandals—they who trample the head of the poor into the dust of the earth, and push the afflicted out of the way; father and son go in to the same girl, so that my holy name is profaned; they lay themselves down beside every altar on garments taken in pledge; and in the house of their God they drink wine bought with fines they imposed (Amos 2:6b-8).

Amos proclaimed that they were not worshipping the true God, but a god of their own making. The God that Amos knew, the God whose message is consistent throughout the Bible, is a God who is committed to the poor. There are more than 2,100 verses in the Bible that speak about caring for the poor and vulnerable in society, which includes the widows, the orphans, and the immigrants. The frequency of this scriptural injunction to care for the disenfranchised is second only to the commands not to commit idolatry. Together, they are the constant reminder to live out the Great Commandment of which Jesus spoke. When a scribe asked Jesus which is the first commandment,

> Jesus answered, "The first is, 'Hear, O Israel: the Lord our God, the Lord is one; you shall love the Lord your God with all your heart, and with all your soul, and with all your mind, and with all your strength.' The second is this, 'You shall love your neighbor as yourself.' There is no other commandment greater than these." (Mark 12:29-31).

God is not pleased with the mere externals of religious observance; after all, God looks on the heart (1 Samuel 16:7). Isaiah 58:6-7 defines true religious practices that please God:

> Is not this the fast that I choose: to loose the bonds of injustice, to undo the thongs of the yoke, to let the oppressed go through, and to break every yoke? Is it not to share your bread with the hungry, and bring the homeless into your house; when you see the naked, to cover them, and not hide from your own kin?

Jesus said that what we do to the least of these—the hungry, the thirsty, the immigrant, the naked, the sick, and the imprisoned—we do to him (Matthew 25:34-46). Jesus was not talking about hungry spiritually, thirsty spiritually, naked spiritually, imprisoned spiritually. Yes, all of these apply, but I believe Jesus was talking about hungry physically, thirsty physically, naked physically, and imprisoned physically.

Jesus' ministry, and likewise ours, is to the whole person; salvation comes to the whole person; *shalom* is for the whole person. We cannot insist that only preaching the gospel matters and relegate social justice issues to secular society. Can the top of a hand be separated from the palm of a hand and still be a hand? Just like a coin has two sides, evangelism, the bringing of the Good News, has two sides—the spoken words and the acted works. One cannot be done to the exclusion of the other.

James said it well:

> What good is it, my brothers and sisters, if you say you have faith but do not have works? Can faith save you? If a brother or sister is

naked and lacks daily food, and one of you says to them, "Go in peace; keep warm and eat your fill," and yet you do not supply their bodily needs, what is the good of that? So faith by itself, if it has no works, is dead. (James 2:14-17).

Jesus' ministry consisted of not only teaching and preaching, but healing and feeding; if we are to follow in our Lord's footsteps, we can do no less.

Our Baptist Legacy

Our Baptist foremothers and forefathers have set an example for us. Lottie Moon (1840–1912) was a missionary to China during a particularly tumultuous time in Chinese history. She preached the gospel in the interior of China where few Western missionaries cared to go. She started schools for girls and women, attending to their needs and providing them with opportunities that Chinese society would not afford its females. She loved the Chinese people so much that she shared freely all that she had and literally starved to death in order to feed the hungry people around her.

Mina Everett (1854–1932) was the first single woman appointed by the Foreign Mission Board of the Southern Baptist Convention. Although her tenure in Brazil was cut short due to illness, she remembered and promoted missions efforts for Brazil. She sold her possessions, including her beloved horse, and lived on a very meager budget in order to give all she could to missions. She loved the Hispanic people of Texas and became a member of a Spanish Baptist church. She was vocal about the equality that women should have with men in matters of service to the kingdom of God and suffered criticism and ostracism by powerful male Baptist pastors. She was a pioneer in many aspects of mission work to ethnic groups, specifically to Hispanic missions in Texas and overseas.

Anne Luther Bagby (1859–1942) and her husband, William, served as missionaries to Brazil for sixty-one years. As with the two aforementioned Baptist women pioneers in missions, Anne started schools and cared for the poor in Brazil. These three brave women did not let gender-based constraints hinder what they perceived to be preaching a full gospel, one that is not only in words, but also in deeds.

Among our Baptist forefathers who showed by their life and work their concern for social justice and social ministry was Walter Rauschenbusch (1861–1918). He was the theologian who gave voice to the need of praxis in the spreading of the gospel, calling Christians to work to transform and make better the society in which they live.

Clarence Jordan (1912–1969) was a Greek New Testament scholar who sought to live out the Christian life as he envisioned Jesus would want, in a community that recognized the equality of all persons regardless of race and color, and to promote harmonious living with nature. The result of his vision was the founding of an interracial Christian community named the Koinonia Farm near Americus, Georgia. He greatly influenced Millard Fuller, who later founded Habitat for Humanity.

The most famous of our Baptist forebears who championed social justice was Martin Luther King Jr. (1929–1968). Dr. King was pivotal in the peaceful resistance of racial prejudice and persecution during the late 1950s to mid-1960s. He is rightly hailed as the father of the Civil Rights Movement. His vision for a future where everyone will be treated with dignity and respect, when all people will be judged by their character and not by the color of their skin, is far from being complete.

Much work remains to build the kingdom of God on earth. As Christians we must get to work, for until there is justice, there is no love, not the kind of love Jesus demonstrated that embraces even the vilest among us. "How does God's love abide in anyone who has the world's goods and sees a brother or sister in need and yet refuses to help? Little children, let us love, not in words or speech, but in truth and action" (1 John 3:17-18). My brothers and sisters, let us be doers of the Word and not merely hearers; let us demonstrate the good news of Jesus Christ and not merely talk about it; let us care for the whole person and, in the process, provoke one another to love and good works (Hebrews 10:24).

CHAPTER 6

A SERMON ON THE BAPTIST DISTINCTIVE OF
Christian Mission

Grace for All People in All Places

AMY E. JACOBER

Acts 13:47

The first time the Bible really seemed to leap beyond the pages of paper and ink for me, I was in Africa. I was awed at the sight of a farmer plowing with oxen yoked together. Families lived in villages with elders respected and water drawn at dawn. Goats and guinea fowl were everywhere, and hospitality reigned supreme. Standing under the most perfect, giant shade tree I could imagine, I was both impressed and humbled as a series of drumbeats brought people walking toward us for more than an hour.

When a large enough crowd gathered, songs and prayers broke out. Dancing followed. A woman threw her arms around me, and I was held by her strong hands on my shoulders with her radiant face studying mine. Her eyes were brilliant, and she called for a translator. She told me that it was about time that I had come. She said that while they loved their missionary brothers, they had wondered where the women were. She told me that they had been blessed by Wycliffe Bible Translators less than five years earlier, receiving Scripture in their own language. As they poured over Scripture, seeking to establish a church, they came to the conclusion that God desired a church mother and father to be in leadership. As they understood Scripture and the presence of the Holy Spirit, she explained to me the equality of men and women as those chosen by God to serve in every facet of the church. She was the mother of this church. She asked me why it had taken so many years for a woman to come to them when they learned this within a few short years. I had no answers. I had no explanation. I knew that many missionaries over the centuries had indeed been female, but in this one small village in northern Ghana, I was the first they had met. I did not even think of myself as a missionary. I was a youth leader taking teenagers on a mission trip. In my mind, that hardly made me a missionary. In the mind of that church mother, I was. When I returned home, I could not stop talking about that experience and my whole time in Ghana.

That tree in Ghana became a memorial of sorts for me. I have a picture of it from a distance. I have never been back in person, but in my mind I have returned a thousand times. Place is important. Places define moments in our lives, holding as precious treasures the activities that passed through them. Recalling or revisiting a place transports us in our minds to previous moments of significance: the place where you were born, the place where you had your first kiss, the place where you first had your heart broken, the place where you were when you learned that a loved one had died, the place where you were when you first heard of the tragedy of 9/11, the place where you find rest and peace, and most importantly, the place where you met the Lord.

Place grounds us. It offers the fertile ground in which we may take root and lay a foundation for life. It offers a tangible reminder that God has created us in particularity. Our location, our culture, and the time in which we live are important. Place also gives a point of departure and potential destination. A few years ago I read a book by Mindy Thompson Fullilove that literally gave language to me to explain some of what I sensed deep within. It is called *Root Shock*. Her research centers on displacement after urban renewal. Her principles, however, transcend her original subject. She spoke of being rooted in a place, of those who developed a sense of belonging that gave them security to venture far. Interestingly, most people cannot identify this rootedness until they are out of it. It is as we come into contact with a place, with a culture, with beliefs and community other than our own that we begin to recognize our own. This is not unlike

Immanuel Kant's "I-Thou." As a woman of faith, I am blessed to have not only a place where I am rooted, but also a person in whom I am rooted. We live in a world filled with sojourners passing through. Increasingly, we are a mobile people, seeking connectedness and community. Jesus Christ offers grounding when the world cannot.

Still, we spend a great deal of time choosing places for significant events. There is an entire industry around choosing the location for a wedding. Graduations are held in significant settings. Inaugurations are held in stately forums. Even in the mundane world of real estate, the most sacred of phrases is "location, location, location."

Paul knew this. Antioch was not a destination chosen simply out of convenience. Antioch was a city of historic importance in the Roman Empire by the time he was to visit: beautiful, buzzing with commerce, filled with luxury, the capital of Syria, at the intersection of caravan routes. It was a collection of the "see and be seen," of those who were viewed with importance in a mixture of communities ranging from relocated Athenians to autonomous Jews living in a southern quarter of the city. It was a prime location both in need of the gospel and poised to be an influential presence for Christ if the gospel were to take root. It was a strategic location.

Though Paul began his missionary journey here, I have another location in mind. I mentioned that I do have a place that grounds me. Anyone who knows me knows that if I were not in ministry, my second career choice would be an Arizona tour guide. I love my home state. I love its very contours. I never feel more settled or grounded than when I am within its borders. The smell of creosote in the air just before a rain, hikes from the top of the state to the bottom, the red rocks of Sedona, and fry bread cooking outside of San Xavier or the Grand Canyon—it is the only place I can be where life just seems to make sense.

I came to know Christ at a Baptist camp up on the Mogollon Rim. It is also in this place that I first remember hearing the word *missionary*. Our speaker at children's camp was a recent college graduate who had just returned from Thailand and was on her way to seminary. With all of my fourth-grade curiosity mustered, I sat spellbound as she talked of traveling to places so far away that I did not even know where they were on a map. The entire group of campers sat mesmerized in a circle on the floor in the mess hall—no small miracle for kids that age. Chopsticks were passed out with bowls of popcorn. She explained that sometimes we have to work hard and do unfamiliar things in order to reach out to new friends with the love of Jesus. It was a simple message. It was a message I still recall. I also still eat popcorn with chopsticks!

But let us get back to Paul. He was on his first missionary journey, ordained by the Holy Spirit through the church at Antioch in Syria, and he was traveling with John Mark and Barnabas. Departing from Antioch, they went to Cyprus, Perga, Antioch in Pisidia (yes, there was more than one Antioch), Iconium, Lystra, Derbe, back to Perga, and then to Attalia before finally returning to Syrian Antioch.

Remember how I could not stop talking about my trip to Ghana went I got back? You know what that is like. You have known someone who had an incredible experience and can talk about nothing else. It crops up in every conversation. This person somehow makes the experience fit into every potential subject, sharing it not only with you, but also with church members, coworkers, store clerks, anyone and everyone who will listen. This person cannot stop talking about that "incredible life-changing experience." This is good, though sometimes annoying. Even more difficult, it is not always well received.

In Acts 13:13-52 we catch a glimpse of Paul and Barnabas sharing their life-changing experience with the church in Pisidian Antioch (John Mark had returned to Jerusalem after Perga). And share they did. Paul was no shrinking violet, and he had a story to tell. He must have been bursting at the seams—empowered by the Spirit, emboldened by experience. Although his calling was to share the gospel with the Gentiles, Paul would not deny his heritage. He spoke first to Jews in the synagogue, drawing on the history of God's dealings with Israel to tell of sin and its consequences and of forgiveness and freedom through the crucifixion and resurrection of Jesus Christ. After listening, many Jews and Jewish converts encouraged Paul and Barnabas to continue in the grace of God and to speak again. But by the time Paul preached his message again a week later, he and Barnabas had become the talk of the town, and almost the whole city gathered to hear them. And at the sight of this huge crowd of Gentiles gathered to hear Paul, the Jews became jealous, and so they contradicted him.

Paul and Barnabas's response to this opposition is what captures my attention: "It was necessary that the word of God should be spoken first to you. Since you reject it and judge yourselves to be unworthy of eternal life, we are now turning to the Gentiles. For so the Lord has commanded us, saying, 'I have set you to be a light for the Gentiles, so that you may bring salvation to the ends of the earth'" (Acts 13:46-47).

Paul and Barnabas, excited about all that God has done, had come to Antioch to share the good news. They long for those in each community to have the same relationship with Christ that they have been proclaiming to others. Sadly, there are those who reject the good news. Paul and Barnabas turn to the Gentiles not for lack of caring about the Jews in Antioch, but rather because of having been rejected and because of their calling to declare what has to be.

In Acts 13:47 Paul is quoting from Isaiah 49:6. This is not the place to discuss whether Paul (via Luke) was quoting from the Hebrew Bible or the Greek Septuagint, but we can notice something interesting about both the Hebrew and Septuagint texts of Isaiah 46:9 and Paul's use of the verse in Acts 13:47. It has a double accusative: "I will give you as a light to the nations" (Isaiah 49:6); "I have set you to be a light for the Gentiles" (Acts 13:47). This means that we *are* a light to the nations—not could be, not should be, not can be. It is not our job to figure out if we are a light to the nations. We are. It is our job to figure out what this looks like.

Paul is letting the people of Antioch know that not only have they, Paul and Barnabas, been established as a light, but so too have all those who follow God. Again, it is stated not as a possibility, but as a fact. It is what has happened. Whether they like it or not, whether they chose it or not, they are set to be the bearers of the gospel even to the ends of the earth. This is no insignificant statement. It is a profound encouragement for a people who too often were surrounded with judgments of their being unworthy of salvation.

In Acts 14:24-28 we read of Paul and Barnabas returning to the point of their commissioning in Syrian Antioch. They reported to those who sent them, doing so, I imagine, with gratitude and conviction. They shared how God had opened the door for faith to Gentiles all along the way. Nothing more is said of their return or report. Based on my experience with many missionaries today, I can only assume that it was a bittersweet report, with the missionaries both sharing experiences with their senders and calling them to a deeper commitment in their own daily lives as well as to those who have not yet heard the good news.

Many of us live in that space as though we are unworthy of God's salvation. It is strange how quickly we will tell others that God's love is for everyone, that there is no sin, no matter how awful, that can separate you from God. And yet sometimes we wonder if that applies to us, that maybe we have cornered the market on sin, sin too egregious to be overturned. The arrogance and foolishness of such thinking is astonishing. I am not saying that we should view ourselves as a spotless gift of God to the world (as John the Baptist said, "I am not the Christ"), but rather that we should view God as great enough to extend grace even in the most seemingly impossible of situations.

When the Gentiles in Antioch heard this news, they embraced it, rejoicing and glorifying God. Similar to Paul and Barnabas, they began to share their life-changing experiences with others, and the word of the Lord was being spread throughout the region (Acts 13:49). Sadly, I am hard pressed to think of the last time I heard someone sharing God's word and was moved to run out immediately to share it with others around me. I thank the Lord that there are others who are much more sensitive, more attuned to the calling of God than I am.

What would it mean for you to be told plainly that you are set, established, as a light for the world in order to bear witness and bring salvation to the ends of the earth? You are. Can you sense the intensity of this realization? Do you rejoice at this call? Go out, be who you have been created to be as a light in this world! We are barraged by messages that seek to crush us, to make us feel unworthy, to remove the confidence of Christ and replace it with the insecurity of the world. This was never God's intent, never God's hope. Listen to the one who created you, who knows you best, who knows that you have something to offer in this world with an impact for eternity. It may mean change in your life. It may mean a few minor renovations or a complete overhaul. Look into the corners of your life, repent from sin, celebrate that you are God's child, and claim your place as what you have been created to be, a bringer of salvation to the ends of the earth.

Be forewarned: this is no easy task. Paul and Barnabas, after preaching good news in Pisidian Antioch, were persecuted and driven out of town by those who took a dim view of their life-changing experience. But Paul and Barnabas knew that their task was unchanged and worth the effort. And so they "shook the dust off their feet" and moved on to Iconium and then Lystra, where they received the same mixed reaction. No matter: they were doing that for which God had set them. Their task, though difficult, was well worth the effort—a light to the Gentiles, salvation to the ends of the earth.

There was a time in Christian history when the notion of missions, of actually traveling to the ends of the earth, was thought of as a historical reality to be remembered, celebrated but not imitated. People viewed this kind of action to be a special calling, not one for which they were qualified or prepared. Sadly, we also have a history of not doing missions well. We cannot move forward if we do not acknowledge the colonialistic manner in which we spread Westernized culture with the same fervor with which we brought the gospel. William Carey ushered in a change to that approach, and missions have never been the same.

Raised in the Church of England, influenced by a fellow cobbler's apprentice, William Carey was baptized in the Baptist church in 1783. Pastoring within a decade, he wrote a manifesto titled *An Enquiry into the Obligations of Christians to Use Means for the Conversion of the Heathens.* I doubt that the title of this book would fly today, but the conviction within its pages changed the face of modern missions. Carey was convinced that Matthew 28:18-20 is not merely a historical artifact; rather, it is a call for all believers and the natural progression of faith. Carey formed the Baptist Missionary Society to send and support those willing to go to the ends of the earth. It was the beginning of cooperative missions efforts as we know them today. Carey took up the call with a first appointment to

India, to which he traveled with his wife and children. William Carey and his family sacrificed all to live out what they had been established to be: a light for the Gentiles bringing the salvation of Christ.

This began the next centuries of Baptist dedication to missions. Soon to follow was the other famous Carey, Lott Carey, who was one of the first black missionaries and the first American Baptist missionary to the continent of Africa.

Mission, then, is a central part of Baptist identity; some would say that it *is* our identity. In particular, Baptists as a people choose to cooperate with one another to accomplish this task. A veritable who's who of Baptist missions exists, including Jim and Elisabeth Elliot, Adoniram and Ann Hasseltine Judson, Lottie Moon, and Annie Armstrong. Beyond these well-known missionaries, Baptists have a long history of faithful servants choosing mission as a way of life, some through vocational missions, others bivocational. Their lives are reminders for us as we realize what God has established us to be: a city on a hill, a beacon of light. We have been created as a shining light, bringing the way of salvation for all the people of the world.

I was charged with looking at the Baptist distinctive of missions in this sermon. Perhaps we are tempted to look at this with the arrow pointing the wrong way. That is, when we say "distinctive," we think "exclusive." So when someone says "missions," we think "Baptist." Thank God that we share this effort with others seeking to build the kingdom. It is better to reverse the arrow, so that when we say "Baptist," we think "missions."

As Baptists, we have much to be rejoice in. We are a people who are committed to God's word, who celebrate gospel proclamation, who hold fast to the importance of baptism, who serve God by serving others. We also are a people who, whenever our name is mentioned, cannot help but think of missions. This is something to celebrate. This is something that reminds us of who we are: given by God as a light to bring salvation to the ends of the earth.

Ecclesiology

Believers' Church, Congregational Polity, Christian Calling, and the Autonomy of the Local Congregation

In 1611 Thomas Helwys wrote his famous treatise, "A Declaration of Faith," in which he defined the ecclesiology of his small band of newly formed Baptists:

> [T]he Church of Christ is a company of faithful people . . . separated from the world by the word and Spirit of God . . . being knit unto the Lord and one unto another by Baptism . . . upon their own confession of faith . . . and sins . . . [T]hough in respect of Christ, the Church be one . . . yet it consists of different particular congregations . . . [each] of which congregation[s], though [the members] be but two or three, have Christ given to them, with all the means of their salvation . . . [Each of which] [is] the Body of Christ . . . and the whole Church.[1]

What is evident from this early Baptist statement of faith is that Baptists understood the church as both universal and local. However, the local church expression is made up of a voluntary membership, which in turn decides its ministry as the local expression of Christ's body. Such an understanding requires Baptists today to study the meaning of a "believers' church," of congregational polity, of calling for its leaders, and the importance of local church autonomy.

Believers' Church

For Baptists, the church is comprised of those who have personally appropriated the Christian faith and who willingly carry out their Christian responsibilities through their faith in Christ. Personal faith, then, is a condition for church membership. Baptists do recognize the universal church as encompassing all believers in heaven and earth at a particular time or even from the time of Christ to the consummation of all things, but when Baptists use the term *church*, typically they are referring to the local community of gathered believers. Historians have noted that the Baptist tradition derived from the quest for a pure church. As H. Leon McBeth puts it, "They sought a church composed of 'visible saints,' that is, true believers, observing the gospel ordinances and obeying the commands of Christ."[2]

Baptists eschewed the notion that a person is incorporated into the church because of national birthright or familial ties to the congregation. Because Baptists insist upon personal faith, the manifestation of that faith is requisite for church membership. Thus, Baptists have always maintained their understanding of the Christian community to be a believers' church, or as John Smyth first described it in 1608–1609, "a true church of true believers." Such a faith is one that is genuinely confessed and practiced by each member. Edward T. Hiscox observed that Baptists have required four basic conditions for membership: a regenerate heart, a confession of faith, the reception of baptism, and a Christian life.[3] These four qualifications help to ensure the authenticity of each believer's faith in maintaining a genuinely confessing membership.

The principle of a believers' church is arguably at the core of all Baptist distinctives. As William Brackney argues, "Baptist theologians know that the key doctrine in Baptist theology pertains to the church. What Baptists think about the church relates to their view of Christ, Christian witness, and relations to other Christians."[4] Every church that stands for this visible company of saints is a part of the catholic, or universal, church of all the elect of God. In order to preserve this standard, then, the early Baptists insisted that each congregation preach the gospel, properly observe the gospel ordinances, and maintain its personal and corporate responsibilities as Christians through church discipline.[5] Although they recognized that even "the purest Churches under heaven are subject to mixture and error,"[6] they posited the Puritan notion of ecclesial purity as their inexorable goal. Though filled with those who were saints while still sinners, Baptist churches have always maintained the principle of a regenerate church membership through baptism and voluntary church covenants. Thus, in Doug Weaver's sermon on this topic to follow, we see that Baptists were born through a search for a genuine "New Testament church," as they understood it.

Congregational Polity

To parallel the Baptist notion of a voluntary church membership and a responsible egalitarian priesthood of every believer, most Baptist congregations over the last four centuries have supported a form of congregational church government in which every member has a decision-making voice in the matters of the church's ministry. Instead of submitting to the authority of a representative group, Baptists are among those Christians who place the authority of the church in the hands of the entire membership. Naturally, this form of government is expressed differently and with nuance among various Baptist churches. And often the congregations elect deacons, elders, and/or a church council to make some day-to-day decisions on behalf of the whole. Regardless, on the major matters of congregational ministry, most Baptists have delegated decision-making responsibilities to the entire membership. Baptists have interpreted the priesthood of all believers, then, to be a tenet applicable even to their polity, perceiving that authority cannot be surrendered to a bishop or even to a smaller body of elders in the church to do this priestly work on behalf of the others. Instead, each believer bears both personal and corporate responsibility in spiritual matters, and the business of the church is part and parcel of these duties. Thus, the congregation is empowered to carry out its authority in worship, Christian education, and the church meeting.

Norman Maring and Winthrop Hudson describe the purpose of the church meeting:

> The church meeting, then, is the place where the whole church gathers to consider matters of importance to its common life. Some business matters should come before it, but it is not just a "business meeting." Calling it that is a symptom of the restricted conception of its purpose which has come to prevail. The adoption of a budget, the admission of members, and setting of policies fall within its necessary competence, but execution of decisions and policies should be left to the designated boards and committees. The church meeting includes relating worship to the internal life of the church, the personal concerns of its members in daily living, community needs, and public policy.[7]

Biblical evidence for congregational government in the churches is gathered in various New Testament passages. For instance, in Acts 15 the entire church sent Paul and Barnabas to Jerusalem to help settle the question of circumcision. Additionally, the Scriptures indicate that the church in Jerusalem had the apostles, the elders, and the entire congregation select some men to help Paul and Barnabas with this endeavor. Additionally, although in his letters addressed to churches Paul sometimes greets particular leaders (Romans 16:1-15; Colossians 4:15), those letters are written to the churches as a whole. This seems to imply that each church as a whole had authority residing in its membership, a concept beautifully proclaimed in the sermon on this subject by Carol Crawford Holcomb to follow.

Calling

Baptists, like other Protestants, believe that all Christians are called to ministry, most often to the work where God has already placed them. As a priesthood of all believers, the church is comprised of ministers who care for one another and carry out their callings not only within the church but also in their occupations, with their families, and through the other roles they play in life. Nevertheless, Baptists, like most Christians, still understand the special calling placed on certain individuals who are gifted for specialized ministry, most typically in preaching and local church leadership.

The discernment of that call is a process that is enacted both individually and corporately. Like other Christians, Baptists understand that each person whom a congregation might call into professional service is being called not only by the church but especially by God. As Hebrews 5:4 notes: "One does not take the honor upon himself, but he is called by God, just as Aaron was." Thus, candidates for ministry are those who at first felt led into ministry, not only by family, friends, and church but especially by God's leadership and encouragement. Those individuals who believe that God might have placed this role upon them seek the inner assurance of this divine leadership. Healthy churches essentially play the role of Eli to Samuel (1 Samuel 1) by assisting inquirers in discerning and understanding their particular call to ministry. The confirmation of the community of faith is then integral to this process. Norman Maring and Winthrop Hudson note:

Today, when it is common to regard a call to the ministry as strictly a private matter, it is well to remember the importance Baptists have placed upon the church's role in a call. If the ministry belongs ultimately to the whole church of Christ, then it is the responsibility of the particular church to select qualified and gifted persons to act as its representatives in the broader ministry of the whole church.[8]

As autonomous congregations, each Baptist church then ordains those individuals within the church whom they discern are genuinely called by God into ministry. Additionally, individual Baptist congregations call their own ministers whom they determine and feel divinely led to become their own pastors and leaders. And in his sermon to follow, Ralph Douglas West describes the Christian call to ministry and the important role of discernment placed on both the individual and church for each person who might answer that call.

Autonomy of the Local Congregation

A corollary to the principle of congregational polity is the concept of local church autonomy. It follows that if authority rests in the hands of the entire congregation, then the local congregation is the seat of authority. There is no external power exerting authority on the church and no representative group that has final authority, which belongs only to Christ himself. One might argue that local church autonomy is a corporate extension of the freedom of conscience and soul competency celebrated for each individual. One congregation cannot have sway over another. Instead, the local church is self-governing. Each congregation calls its own pastor and determines its own budget. Modern congregations have other churches, associations, and denominational resources to provide help and advice, but these must be limited to voluntary and assisting roles. Some Baptists have suggested in support of this tenet that although the apostles made recommendations and even forcefully urged churches to reform their ways, it was still left to each church to listen and decide what to do.[9]

This is not to imply, however, that Baptist congregations act in isolation from one another, any more than an individual Baptist is to be cloistered from his or her community. This strong warning against isolationist interpretations of this doctrine is underscored in David Wilhite's sermon on this topic to follow. Instead, healthy Baptist con-gregations have always found associations, denominations, ecu-menical projects, and mission agencies in which to participate. Although such participation must never be coerced from outside, churches must work in tandem with larger entities as they recognize the kingdom work of the gospel beyond their own communities and beyond what any one congregation can do alone. William Brackney notes, "Democratic decision-making is thus an important hallmark of Baptist congregational life as individuals express their spiritual competencies in relationship to each other and with Christ in their midst. Similarly, the congregation, acting as a unified spiritual body, voluntarily identifies the external relationships it will maintain in the interest of its mission and outreach."[10] And E. Y. Mullins emphasized that churches must continually understand the importance of their autonomy in their voluntary associations:

> Here we may point out the relation of local Baptist churches to gen-eral Baptist bodies, missionary, educational, and so forth. The lat-ter are not composed of churches but of individuals. Churches may use them or not use them, cooperate with them or refuse to coop-erate with them. In all such cooperation or refusal to cooperate, however, the church neither assumes authority over the general body, nor submits to the authority of that body. The relation is vol-untary on both sides.[11]

Thus, while Baptists have benefited from having an associational spirit and have accomplished much through denominational min-istries, each congregation is free to make its own decisions under the lordship of Christ alone. Christ Jesus is the only high priest, to whom each church is answerable.

Notes

1. Articles 10 and 11 originally cited in William L. Lumpkin, ed., *Baptist Confessions of Faith* (Valley Forge, PA: Judson Press, 1969), 119–120; here cited in T. Furman Hewitt, "The Church," in *A Baptist's Theology*, ed. R. Wayne Stacy (Macon, GA: Smyth & Helwys, 1999), 113.

2. H. Leon McBeth, *The Baptist Heritage: Four Centuries of Baptist Witness* (Nashville: B&H Academics, 1987), 75.

3. Everett C. Goodwin, *The New Hiscox Guide for Baptist Churches* (Valley Forge, PA: Judson Press, 1995), 33.

4. William H. Brackney, *A Capsule History of Baptist Principles* (Atlanta: Baptist History and Heritage Society, 2009), 39.

5. See McBeth, *The Baptist Heritage*, 76.

6. "The Second London Confession," cited in Lumpkin, *Baptist Confessions of Faith*, 285.

7. Norman H. Maring and Winthrop S. Hudson, *A Baptist Manual of Polity and Practice*, rev. ed. (Valley Forge, PA: Judson Press, 1991), 59.

8. Ibid., 113–14.

9. See Millard J. Erickson, *Christian Theology*, 2nd. ed. (Grand Rapids: Baker Academic, 1998), 1089–93.

10. Brackney, *A Capsule History*, 54.

11. E. Y. Mullins, *Baptist Beliefs* (Valley Forge, PA: Judson Press, 1925), 65–66.

Action Steps for the Reader

1. For further reading on Baptist ecclesiology:

Durnbaugh, Donald F. *The Believers' Church: The History and Character of Radical Protestantism.* Scottdale, PA: Herald Press, 1968.

Goodwin, Everett C. *The New Hiscox Guide for Baptist Churches.* Valley Forge, PA: Judson Press, 1995.

Jenson, Matt, and David Wilhite. *Church: A Guide for the Perplexed.* London: T & T Clark International, 2010.

Maring, Norman H., and Winthrop S. Hudson. *A Baptist Manual of Polity and Practice.* Rev. ed. Valley Forge, PA: Judson Press, 1991.

2. Biblical texts for preaching and topical Bible study:

1 Samuel 3:1-10; Matthew 16:15-19; 18:15-20; Acts 2:41-42,47; 5:11-14; 6:3-6; 13:1-3; 14:23,27; 15:1-30; 16:5; 20:28; Romans 1:7; 1 Corinthians 1:2; 3:16; 5:4-5; 7:17; 9:13-14; 12; Ephesians 1:22-23; 2:19-22; 3:8-11,21; 5:22-32; Philippians 1:1; Colossians 1:18; 1 Timothy 3:1-15; 4:14; Titus 1:6-9.

3. Idea for worship:

Experience a "laying on of hands" service as your church commissions missionaries, ministers, or deacons, allowing the entire congregation to participate, representing the spiritual democracy of your church and the local church's responsibility to those whom it freely chooses to ordain.

4. Opportunity for service:

Experience the joy of local church autonomy not only by having your church's missions committee and leadership support service projects and missions work conducted by your denominational boards, but also by serving those in physical and spiritual need in your local community. Remember that Christ sent his disciples to Judea, Samaria, and the ends of the earth. Consider your church as a local outpost of the kingdom of God by finding ways to serve your community as a congregation.

CHAPTER 7

A Stink in Your Nostrils?

C. DOUGLAS WEAVER

Ephesians 4:1-6

Most Baptists will tell you that they do not have a recognizable founder like Martin Luther or John Calvin or John Wesley. The earliest Baptist church was formed over four hundred years ago, in 1609, because the first Baptists believed that a fresh start was necessary. They said that no human founder of a church had proved faithful. No succession from a church founder had produced a pure body of Christ. All so-called Christian churches were corrupted because they did not fully follow the model for a true church outlined in the New Testament. The Puritans had claimed that they were purifying the Church of England and completing the Reformation, but they had failed, primarily in their retention of infant baptism. Consequently, when Englishman John Smyth organized the first Baptist church in Amsterdam, Holland, the search for a pure church, a true church that embodied the New Testament blueprint, was the underlying motive for leaving Puritan Separatism. Smyth wanted to establish *the* New Testament church, and he believed that believer's baptism was the link to the genuine New Testament believers' church model.

This is a good place to hear the story of John Smyth and Thomas Helwys in a little more detail. The Christian journey of John Smyth revealed a constant and restless search for the New Testament church. He was a child of the Protestant Reformation. He grew up in the Church of England and was ordained as an Anglican minister in

1594. He soon became a Puritan within the Anglican Church, hoping to purify the church from its Catholic excesses. In 1606 he became a Separatist Puritan, the most radical branch of Puritans, who decided that the Anglican Church could not be reformed and so the creation of independent nonconforming churches was necessary. Many Separatists, in an environment of harassment and persecution from King James, fled to Holland.

Like other Separatist pastors, Smyth affirmed the idea of the "gathered church," a body of professing believers bound together in a voluntary covenant of faith and obedience. Unlike some Separatists, this gathered church followed congregational polity. Governing authority belonged to the members of the congregation because they were participants in the covenant. The test of a regenerate church membership was a visible faith. Smyth (and other Separatists) wanted a regenerate church to model itself after the New Testament church.

However, Smyth soon decided that his church did not yet model a New Testament congregation. The issue was infant baptism. Traditionally, Separatists had discussed the validity of baptism in the "false" Church of England, but they had not abandoned their infant baptism, in part because they did not want be associated with the "rebaptism" of the Anabaptists, the most maligned group of the Reformation. Separatists also followed the line of thinking that said that children were brought into the church's covenant with God because of the faith of the parents.

Smyth's search for the true church led him to the conclusion that there was no biblical basis for infant baptism. For the church to be genuine, infants must be excluded from membership because they were incapable of expressing faith and repentance, which are the conditions of obedience in God's spiritual covenant with the church. Baptism of believers—those old enough to profess their faith voluntarily—was the New Testament method of constituting a church. The New Testament church, then, was a believers' church. Smyth put it this way in a short confession of faith: "The church is a company of the faithful, baptized after confession of sin and faith, endowed with the power of Christ."

Having finally concluded that no genuine New Testament church existed, in 1609 Smyth disbanded his own congregation of about forty persons, baptized himself by pouring, and then baptized his fellow believers into a new believers' church—what is acknowledged as the first Baptist church in history. Smyth, according to some critics, was now "John the Se-Baptist"!

The Baptist story started with John Smyth, but it quickly shifted to Thomas Helwys, a wealthy layperson in Smyth's congregation who most likely funded the group's journey from England to Amsterdam. Not long after this first Baptist church had formed, Helwys led a split involving ten persons from Smyth's congregation after Smyth pushed the congregation to affiliate with the Mennonites. After learning more about the Mennonites, Smyth had decided that baptizing himself was a mistake. The Mennonites appeared to be a genuine believers' church formed on the basis of believer's baptism. Smyth thus opted for the principle of "succession"; that is, if a genuine believers' church existed, then baptism should be received from it. Thomas Helwys strongly opposed the necessity of succession to validate the existence of a genuine church; he pointed to the nonbaptized John the Baptist, who preached the necessity of New Testament believer's baptism for repentance. According to Helwys, Smyth's opting for ministerial succession was a reversion to Jewish ceremonialism. Succession was an Old Testament practice not binding upon New Testament believers. Helwys insisted that the creation of a New Testament church was dependent only upon faithfulness to biblical instructions.

In 1612 Helwys and his small group returned to England and established the first Baptist church on English soil at Spitalfield outside London. In a confessional statement Helwys wrote, in words similar to Smyth's, that the "church of Christ is a company of the faithful people separated from the world by the Word and Spirit of God being knitted unto the Lord and one unto another by Baptism upon their confession of the faith." In England, the young congregation emphasized many features that for four centuries have continued to describe a believers' church identity for most Baptists.

1. The church must be faithful to the Scriptures and to the Spirit of God.
2. A church should be a believers' church, which necessarily excludes infants from membership.

3. Membership in a believers' church is based on personal confession of faith and believer's baptism. Like Smyth, Helwys wrote that members should be received "by baptism upon the confession of faith and sins" because this is the "primitive institution" of the New Testament church.
4. The believers' church is characterized by the independence of each local church from other religious figures or bodies. Helwys put it this way: because "each church has Christ," "no church ought to challenge any prerogative over any other."
5. The believers' church has congregational church governance. Believers are knitted to God and to each other as a company of the faithful and thus are called to be separate from worldly ways.
6. While the believers' church is a community of believers knitted together, at the same time it must also have religious liberty for all persons. Each person must be able to read the Bible and is free to follow God according to the dictates of his or her conscience under the lordship of Christ.

No doubt, these earliest Baptists believed that they embodied the one faith and one baptism of Ephesians 4:5.

In the decades and centuries after Smyth and Helwys, Baptists continued to emphasize these elements of a believers' church. They always tried to root their ecclesiology in the Scripture. So, Baptists turned to Acts 2:37-42 to emphasize that baptism came after confession of sin. They also noted that the Ethiopian eunuch in Acts 8:26-40 was baptized after he believed. Thus, they confidently preached that infants were not a part of the church; infants could not freely believe.

Baptists also rooted their congregationalism and local church independence in the Scriptures. Congregational polity was tied to the focus on the priesthood of all believers in 1 Peter 2:4-10. If everyone is a priest, then surely all are equal and have a voice in the affairs of the church. Baptists also did not find a leadership hierarchy in the New Testament. They did not find it in the letter to the Philippians, which Paul addressed to "the saints . . . with the bishops and deacons," and they did not find it in the Corinthian church, where spiritual gifts were flying everywhere.

Save for a little while your evaluation of whether these Baptists interpreted the New Testament in ways you find acceptable. It is easy to pick at some of the proof texts. And of course it is easy for us to pick at any who too confidently identify their group with the "one Lord, one faith, one baptism" focus of Ephesians 4:5. So, try to focus for now on the fact that Baptists contended that a believers' church is characterized by freedom rooted in Scripture. Each believer had to freely confess sin and profess belief in Christ, each believer had to be baptized to signify that belief, and each church was free to govern its affairs as it believed God's word and Spirit were leading it.

This freedom to be a believers' church—free from state control and free from ecclesiastical hierarchy—did not mean, however, that one believers' church held identical beliefs with another believers' church or implemented its beliefs in the same way. Actually, it might be better to talk about the Baptist distinctive of believers' *churches.*

Think about the following examples, all of which occurred in the first several decades of Baptist life in the seventeenth century. Most believers' churches began insisting that believer's baptism by immersion was the biblical method of establishing a church, and it was the only proper method of baptism. They argued that baptism had to be done by immersion because they translated the biblical word *baptizō* as "dip." And the baptismal imagery of death, burial, and resurrection in Romans 6 pointed to immersion. Based on Hebrews 6:1-2, some, though not all, believers' churches insisted that the church adopt laying on of hands after baptism as a sign of receiving the Holy Spirit. Some, though not all, believers' churches insisted that footwashing was a church ordinance because of Jesus' washing of the disciples' feet in John 13:1-17. Some believers' churches, though not all, insisted that singing was appropriate for believers as long as the words of the songs were from the Bible, but some thought that singing by women defied the biblical injunction for women to keep silent in the church. Some believers' churches, though never a majority, said that the Trinity was not in the Scriptures. Some believers' churches were Arminian, some were Calvinist, and some were mixed.

In subsequent centuries some Baptist believers' churches began to advocate sending missionaries to foreign lands; some believers' churches said that missions were an insult to God, who had predestined certain people to heaven; some believers' churches said that mission boards were nowhere to be found in the Bible and therefore should not be considered a part of the church's work.

One of my favorite examples comes from the mid-seventeenth century and involves the believers' church known as the Seventh Day Baptists. They believed that Christians were to worship on the Sabbath, which is our Saturday. Where in the Bible, these believers asked, does it say to cease following the Ten Commandments, which mandate keeping the Sabbath? So these Seventh Day Baptists worked on Sunday, infuriating other Baptists. If they attended the Sunday service, they refused to take Communion. One church leader had had enough and said to the Seventh Day Baptists, "Do you follow Moses, or do you follow Christ?" The Seventh Day Baptists no doubt were insulted. Their leader responded that the Sunday Christians were treating the Ten Commandments as "a stink in their nostrils." The Seventh Day Baptists challenged the others: if you are going to be a believers' church, then go ahead and believe it all.

We could look at many more examples. The diversity of Baptist believers' churches was and is bewildering. But it should not be surprising, since the Baptist believers' church is rooted in freedom. Think about that. It is actually a bit more in line with what you New Testament exegetes out there have already been thinking, right? Certainly you have been saying to yourself, "Well, there was no New Testament church; there were New Testament churches."

Yes, freedom is at the heart of Baptist believers' churches, but is it too messy and chaotic? For Baptists, is freedom the "stink in their nostrils"? Some say so. Some say that we should put a cap on the freedom by demanding a common creed that goes beyond an affirmation of biblical authority to insist upon certain interpretations of the Bible. If you want a believers' church rather than believers' churches, some insist, then a hierarchy of leaders or an authoritative teaching office is required to insure against the abuse of freedom. Some say that freedom in Baptist believers' churches has far too long focused on individual freedom and soul competency, and that freedom is communal but not individual. Community is in; the individual is out.

E. Y. Mullins, an influential Baptist theologian of the twentieth century, acknowledged the dangers of freedom, but he insisted that it is at the heart of being a believers' church and thus at the heart of being a Baptist Christian. Freedom is necessary for an individual to respond directly to God's offer of grace for salvation. Conversion cannot be forced or accepted by proxy. Freedom is the DNA of soul competency. Freedom is also necessary for each congregation to respond directly to God because history has shown that state-sponsored religion and established clergy persecuted dissenters for failing to accept the beliefs of the ruling majority. Baptist believers' churches should use their freedom to cooperate with other Christians, but the cooperation must be rooted in freedom, not coercion or compulsion.

Mullins knew that Baptists were not all the same; he knew that freedom meant diversity, but he thought that genuine belief impelled persons to be part of the spiritual community Scripture called "the body of Christ." He asserted that the church was a spiritual community of individual believers bound together by a common personal experience of God's salvific grace, a common commitment to the Bible as the sole authority for religious faith and practice, and a common commitment to the lordship of Christ.

Like Baptist pioneers before him, Mullins tried to balance the potential excess of individual freedom by arguing for local church autonomy, a historic Baptist identity marker. This was his way of saying what Thomas Helwys and John Smyth said: believers are in covenant with God individually and are knit together in covenant with each other. It was "individual in community." This combination is what he considered to be the example of New Testament faith.

So, how does the believers' church allow for freedom but also acknowledge that freedom can be abused? Each church allowed all believers to have a voice, to voice the dissent of individual conscience, but then the congregation as a whole functioned as a Baptist bishop and judged whether the dissent was accepted: was it biblically sound? The dissent must not be silenced nor the conscience stifled, because Christian identity ultimately is eschatological. Mullins followed early Baptists such as Thomas Helwys, John Clarke, and Isaac Backus, who declared that "Only God was Lord of the Conscience," and thus the individual believer must be free to follow his or her conscience this side of heaven because, at the last judgment, it will be only the believer standing face to face with God. Clearly, state-sponsored established churches and church hierarchies will not be there to help, but not even a good local church could assist at that point. If you believe in a last judgment as described in the New Testament, the Baptist tradition declared, you had better preserve individual freedom, no matter how risky it might be to an orderly church life.

Ecclesiology is tied to eschatology. Freedom for the individual and freedom for the group work together. Some folks today seem to think that it is all community and no individual. It is almost as if, based on the amount of time spent on the topic, communal ecclesiology has replaced Christology or the Trinity as the focus of Christianity. But the early Baptists insisted that the Christian life—the life of the church—was both personal and communal.

Personal: Jesus says that there is joy in heaven when one sinner repents (Luke 15:7).

Communal: Jesus fed the five thousand (Matthew 14:13-21; Mark 6:32-44; Luke 9:10-17; John 6:1-15).

Personal: Paul says, "I have been crucified in Christ; and it is no longer I who live, but it is Christ who lives in me" (Galatians 2:19-20).

Communal: Paul says, "Work out your own salvation with fear and trembling" (Philippians 2:12), and his Greek verb and pronoun are in the plural.

Personal: Paul says, "I can do all things through him who strengthens me" (Philippians 4:13).

Communal: Paul says, "For in the one Spirit we were all baptized into one body. . . . Now you are the body of Christ and individually members of it" (1 Corinthians 12:13,27).

It is not either/or, but rather both/and—personal and communal. It was necessary tension. It was eschatological ecclesiology. If that is like a stink in your nostrils, then being Baptist can be pretty discomforting.

The next time you tell someone about Baptists as a believers' church, admit that Baptists are a messy lot and talk about believers' churches. Admit the flawed attempts at being church as you find them. You will find some. But Baptists, at their best, amid their diversity, share a common individual faith commitment in Christ, a common attachment to the body of Christ, a common authority in the Scriptures, and a common commitment to Jesus Christ as Lord—the only Lord for the individual conscience, and the only Lord for the church.

CHAPTER 8

Congregational Polity

A Recipe for Anarchy?

CAROL CRAWFORD HOLCOMB

Acts 6:1-6; 13:1-3

We were waiting for the storm. It was inevitable. The room was oddly quiet as deacons shuffled in, nodding their greetings and taking their places in the metal folding chairs placed against the walls. We stared at each other, waiting for someone to speak. We were gathered because the pastor search committee had made a decision. The name that they recommended to this small church in central Texas was unmistakably that of a woman, and the news had spread like wildfire. The rumor mill began to grind. Some of the church members protested and insisted that the deacons disband the committee. So, the deacons gathered in a Sunday school classroom on that hot August afternoon to discuss the "problem." Some of us held our breath. We were waiting for the storm.

Finally, an older deacon broke the silence. "Well, I am furious!" he roared. "The decisions of a search committee should be kept private until the committee submits their formal recommendation to the church! This is awful." Slowly, deacon after deacon began to express anger that some committee members had broken faith and whispered the news prematurely. In one corner, the patriarch of the church sat in silence. At age eighty-six, he was the senior deacon in the room and one of the most respected members of the church. He sat perched on the front of his folding chair, leaning slightly forward on a long wooden cane. His piercing blue eyes gazed intently around the room as he quietly absorbed the conversation. Most of us wanted and needed to hear his opinion. "Well, I will tell you this," he said in a strong, steady voice. "If we dissolve this committee, we might as well all go home." He banged his cane on the floor for emphasis. "The church appointed that committee to search for a pastor. We trusted them to do this. They have the right to bring any recommendation that they choose. We all have the right to vote however we choose. If we want to vote against their choice, we can do that. Any one of us can vote down their choice. But if we work around this committee, then we might as well all go home. We are not Baptists anymore."

I looked around the room perplexed and a little disoriented. The senior adults were angry, but not because the committee had chosen a woman. They were angry because the process was being tampered with. They were angry about a broken trust, about gossip, and "political wire pulling." None of them pledged to vote for a female candidate. In fact, some of them stated clearly that they might vote against her. For them, this was not about women in ministry; this was about church unity and good order. For this group of deacons, Baptist identity meant a democratic process—transparency, vigorous debate, mutual trust, faithful committee work, and, ultimately, a vote. It is remarkable that in central Texas a breach of due process sparked more outrage than the idea of women in ministry. Why this passionate concern for a proper method of church governance (polity)?

If we are honest about it, the mention of church polity evokes little more than a stifled yawn from most of us. Advertise church polity as the sermon topic in the bulletin, and you can virtually hear the corporate sigh. Perhaps this is a generational issue. Maybe our pronounced ambivalence toward matters of governance stems from a false distinction between "business" matters and "spiritual" matters, as though the governance of the church is somehow unconnected to the work of the kingdom of God. In truth, the everyday matters of the church, from choosing deacons and pastors to organizing the budget, are profoundly spiritual issues that will shape how well the church functions as the body of Christ.

Why do Baptists follow congregational polity? Certainly, other faith traditions have employed different models of church governance. One model, known as episcopal polity, was practiced by the

Roman Catholic Church and the Church of England when the first Baptist church was established. According to the episcopal system, the authority for the life of the church began with Jesus and the apostles. Bishops preserved the teaching of the apostles and then passed the teaching on to younger bishops, who in turn passed the teaching on to the next generation. This concept of church authority, called "apostolic succession," emerged in the second century when the church needed to defend its teaching against various heresies. Early church writers argued that the church's teaching was valid because the apostles had been taught by Jesus himself and transferred that teaching to church leaders. Paul's admonition to Timothy to "entrust" his teachings to reliable leaders (2 Timothy 2:2) provides a biblical injunction for the maintenance of apostolic instruction. Thus, the bishops are the successors of the apostles, and as such, they preserve the teachings of the apostles and keep them pure for the church. In an episcopal system local congregations remain in good standing with the church if they conform to the teachings of the bishops.

A second model of church government is representative government or presbyterian polity. A local congregation elects presbyters or elders to govern the life of the church. Each congregation then chooses representatives to serve on a synod that governs member churches. Although the congregations are not entirely self-governing, they do have a voice in the composition of the governing body. Like the episcopal system, presbyterian polity draws upon New Testament concepts of church elders. For example, Paul and Barnabas appoint elders to the church at Antioch (Acts 14:23), and Paul describes to Titus the qualifications of an elder (Titus 1:5-9). These differing models of church order reveal that faithful believers disagree on the interpretation of Scripture. In each case, however, their polity grows naturally from their reading of Scripture. Baptists are no different.

The senior adults in our church imbibed their Baptist identity from a generation of leaders who did not hesitate to celebrate the democratic nature of Baptist identity. Early twentieth-century Baptists, for good or ill, trumpeted congregational polity as the hallmark of the Baptist faith. They believed that a church should be governed by its members. In a recent speech, sociologist Nancy Ammerman stated, "Baptists have become inextricably linked to the political theory of democracy." She went on to argue that soul competency and congregationalism conveyed civic skills to indigenous communities. Because Baptists have dispersed their pattern of organizing through their extensive missionary work, she noted, they have inadvertently shaped democracies around the world. "But Baptists started with theology," Ammerman asserted, "not political theory."[1]

Congregational polity flows naturally from Baptist theology. Many issues contribute to our church order, but four interrelated concepts stand out. First of all, early Baptist leaders sought to establish their churches according to a New Testament pattern. Like other Protestant Reformers, they viewed the Bible as the sole authority for faith and practice. They believed, based upon their reading of the text, that churches should be self-governing, as depicted in Acts 13:1-3, where the church at Antioch commissions Barnabas and Saul. Baptists pointed to the choosing of the seven deacons in Acts 6:1-6, the lists of gifts for ministry in 1 Corinthians 12:8-11, and the qualifications for leaders in 1 Timothy 3 as evidence that church members decided key issues as a community.[2] Based on these and other passages, our Baptist forbears concluded that believers should be free to gather a church, choose their own ministers, and discipline members without asking permission from a church official or civil authority. The First London Confession of 1677 states that "every Church has power given them from Christ . . . to choose to themselves meet persons into the office of Pastors, Teachers, Elders, Deacons."[3] Often Baptists refer to this principle of local congregational control as church autonomy. Baptist theologian Stanley Grenz points out that the titles of denominations tend to reflect their polity. "Whereas most groups speak of a national or international church (e.g., the Presbyterian Church), Baptists generally employ terms such as 'conference' or 'convention' of churches," says Grenz. "There is no Baptist Church, only Baptist churches."[4] Baptist churches are not hardwired together; they are independent and autonomous.

A commitment to the authority of Scripture led Baptists to a second conviction: a believers' church. During the Reformation Era scholars produced many new translations in modern languages. At last, lay people could look to the Scriptures directly for guidance in faith. Most early Baptist leaders were not trained clergy. A church record from 1640 mentions a butcher, a blacksmith, a housewife, and a young minister who "covenanted together" to form a Baptist church. When these common people read Scripture, they found no biblical grounds for infant baptism. Furthermore, they scandalized the established churches by insisting that only those who had professed faith in Christ and submitted to believer's baptism could be members of the church. Edward Barber, an early Baptist leader, insisted that the Lord had raised him, "a poore tradesman," to divulge the glorious truth concerning baptism.[5] These seventeenth-century Baptists were called "dissenters" and were considered to be nonconformists because they did not look to bishop, council, or tradition for their authority to establish a believers' church. With Bible in hand, they baptized one another and covenanted together to form a "pure" church.

Third, Baptists have persistently proclaimed the absolute lordship of Christ. It was through the written text that Martin Luther encountered the living word after a long, anguished spiritual struggle. Though he fasted and prayed, beat his body, and confessed his sins, though he made a pilgrimage to Rome, Luther could find no peace. His superiors suggested that he seek a doctorate in theology and become a professor of Bible at the University of Wittenberg to soothe his troubled soul. (By the way, I would not recommend a doctorate as a cure for spiritual anguish.) Nevertheless, Luther found peace through his study of Scripture. By reading Romans, Luther discovered that all his work to earn the favor of God was meaningless, because the work had been finished by Jesus on the cross. "Justified by faith" liberated Luther and set his life on a different path. In 1518, in a lecture on the psalms, Luther said it this way: "All good things are hidden in the cross and under the cross. . . . Thus I, poor little creature, do not find anything in the Scriptures but Jesus Christ and Him crucified." For Luther, this was the gospel in a nutshell. It is only through Christ that we are made right with God.

Baptists fully embraced justification by faith and refused to allow anyone or anything to trespass on the authority of Christ. The Baptist pleas for religious toleration were rooted in the lordship of Christ. Thomas Helwys died in prison after he dared to inform the British king that his kingdom did not extend to human souls. "Let our Lord Jesus Christ in all his power and Majesty sit upon David's throne," pleaded

Helwys, "and let Christ according to his own wisdom judge his people Israel [the church], and let our Lord the King be his subject."[6] Two years later Baptist Leonard Busher proclaimed, "No king nor bishop can, or is able to command faith; That is the gift of God."[7] Roger Williams was tossed out of the Massachusetts Bay Colony because he denied that any government could legislate matters of faith.

George W. Truett, longtime pastor of the First Baptist Church in Dallas, argued that the lordship of Christ serves as the cornerstone of all Baptist faith and practice. Truett delivered a sermon on the steps of the United States capitol building in 1920. This sermon has become known as a classic presentation of Southern Baptist heritage. As was common in that era, Truett celebrated Baptist polity as the spiritual corollary to political democracy. He insisted that all Baptist beliefs and practices, including congregational polity, hinged upon the lordship of Christ. Some who are embarrassed by the triumphalist tone of the sermon may miss the theological rationale that Truett provided. "That doctrine [lordship of Christ] is for Baptists the dominant fact in all their Christian experience," argued Truett, "the nerve center of all their Christian life, the bedrock of all their church polity, the sheet anchor of all their hopes, the climax and crown of all their rejoicing." "From the germinal conception of the absolute Lordship of Christ," said Truett, "all our Baptist principles emerge. Just as yonder oak came from the acorn, so our many-branched Baptist life came from the cardinal principle of the absolute Lordship of Christ."[8]

Still, how does the lordship of Christ relate to local church governance? For one thing, we look to Christ as the leader of the church. "Christ is the head of the church," Truett continued. "All authority has been committed unto Him, in heaven and on earth, and He must be given the absolute pre-eminence in all things."[9] In his *Essay on the Power of an Association*, Benjamin Griffith asserted that "each particular church hath a complete power and authority from Jesus Christ, to administer all gospel ordinances, . . . and to exercise every part of gospel discipline and church government, independent of any other church or assembly whatever."[10] The power to order the affairs of the church comes directly from Christ.

The authority of Scripture, a believers' church, and the preeminence of Christ lead to a fourth principle that Luther termed "the priesthood of believers" based upon 1 Peter 2:5,9 and Revelation 1:6; 5:10. Nothing should stand between Christ and believers—no pastor, priest, bishop, or government official. Because of Christ's death and resurrection, believers no longer need a priest to speak to God on their behalf. Christians are to be priests to one another, intercede for one another (1 Timothy 2:1-2), and offer themselves as living sacrifices to God (Romans 12:1). Priesthood implies both personal and communal responsibility. A believer has personal access to God through Christ Jesus. Baptists have long affirmed that Christ, through the Holy Spirit, leads believers personally. Ministers of the state churches often laughed at the idea that common people in a congregation could make good decisions about matters of faith. So what made these Baptists think they were capable of making decisions on their own? They did not believe that they were capable on their own. On the contrary, believers could make decisions for Christ because they were made capable by grace through faith. Baptists would use the expression "soul competency" to convey that Christ, through the Holy Spirit, guides believers and equips them for faithful service.

A believers' church requires believer's baptism, which assumes soul competency. Baptist "dissenters" in England asserted that baptism "requires faith as an inseparable condition."[11] Again and again, baptism treatises insisted that faith must precede baptism and that none of this is possible apart from grace. Soul competency does not mean self-sufficiency; rather, it is a gift of God. Every individual has the freedom to hear God's call and to respond to that call in faith because God has provided the opportunity through his grace. Soul competency assumes the presence and power of the Holy Spirit working in the heart of the believer. This much was clear to a wealthy Baptist farmer and wagon maker in Boston over 350 years ago.

In 1655 a Puritan, Thomas Gould, refused to have his infant daughter baptized. Why? Because Gould was a devout churchman; he read his Bible scrupulously, as his ministers had taught him. It troubled his mind that he could find no direct teaching concerning infant baptism. Gould asked for permission to disagree with the church on this one matter. Instead, he was "presented to the County Court by the grand jury of Middlesex County in December 1656, 'for denying baptisme to his child.'"[12] When he obstinately refused to repent, Gould was thrown into prison, where he languished for months on end. Because Gould was well respected in the community and one of the wealthier citizens of the Massachusetts Bay Colony, friends and neighbors finally were able to persuade the authorities to relent. When he returned to his farm, Gould invited a few Baptists and other like-minded men and women to meet in his home for prayer. Not long after, these Puritan believers covenanted together to form a Baptist church.

Because of the Baptist agitations, the governor and council of Boston called for a debate with the Baptists in 1668. The Puritan ministers pressed Gould and his fellow Baptists to explain what authority allowed them to dissent from the majority. The debate boiled down to a question of whether an individual had the right to challenge the tradition of the community. Historian William McLoughlin maintains that the heart of the debate "was a more complicated and far reaching issue: the implicit challenge of the Baptist individualism (through reliance upon the Holy Spirit) to the corporate ideals of Bible Commonwealth."[13] Note the parenthesis of the Holy Spirit. This is the basis of a Baptist understanding of both individualism and community. The authority, the "glue," that holds Baptists in community is the presence of the Holy Spirit in each individual.

The Puritan leadership believed that this was a dangerous doctrine and would lead to fanaticism, individualism, and all manner of chaos. When Gould was pressed further to explain why an individual could dissent, he replied, "Christ dwelleth in no temple but in the heart of the believer." The Puritans rejected this, saying that Christ's words were "I will dwell in *them*" (the community). The Baptists could not be persuaded. "Every man must judge for himself," they argued. "The spirit of God in every Christian tells them whether the other be right in spirit or in form only." If indeed the Puritans were correct and the Spirit indwelled "them" (the collective of the institutional church rather than the individual), then adult baptism would have been superfluous. Adult believer's baptism is predicated on the idea that the Holy Spirit indwells individuals who together constitute the church.

As we noted earlier, after being dismissed from the established churches, Boston Baptists immediately signed a covenant and formed a new community of faith, one bound together by the Holy Spirit.

The same Spirit who guides believers personally calls them into community. Boston Baptists rejected the Puritan conception of the community that would stifle the freedom of the individual to respond to the Holy Spirit. John Russell, the second pastor of the Boston Baptist congregation, referred to this as "tenderness of conscience"—not a conscience informed by a secular individualism, but one made tender by the word of God and guided by the Holy Spirit.

To the Puritans, this was a recipe for anarchy and, frankly, a willy-nilly way to run a church. To the Baptists, it was nothing more than the exercise of their faith in the power of the Spirit of God. As McLoughlin observes, this new Baptist community would not be sustained or expanded on the basis of the ordered means of the New England Way, but rather by the "sporadic, unpredictable, spontaneous" workings of the Holy Spirit. Likewise, their unity hinged upon their shared testimony, a common narrative of how God had extended the riches of his grace to them in Christ Jesus and sealed them with the Holy Spirit.

Still, some of us probably have sat in business meetings and speculated, like the Puritans, that this is a willy-nilly way to run a church. Most would agree that an episcopal or presbyterian church order can be more efficient, more systematic and expeditious. Congregational polity is difficult to implement. When congregational systems grind slowly, it is tempting to find the grass greener on the other side of the baptistery. However, it is important to remember that patterns of church governance should reflect our convictions about Scripture rather than a utilitarian thirst for efficiency. Baptists adopted congregational church order because it harmonizes with a radical commitment to adult believer's baptism and a believers' church. So, how can we better facilitate our polity? I have a few suggestions.

First, congregational order requires an active program of discipleship. Congregational polity hinges upon the participation of the members, the laity. Because of the historic emphasis on the priesthood of all believers, Baptists have long emphasized the importance of each church member reaching out to the world as priest, evangelist, missionary, teacher, minister, servant, and in all endeavors, to be Christ's ambassador. Therefore, it is crucial that Baptist churches pay careful attention to mentoring new believers in the faith and to discipling members so that they may come to "maturity, to the measure of the stature of Christ" (Ephesians 4:13).

Second, congregational order requires a systematic program of education. Christian education is a corollary to discipleship. Discipleship is following Christ. Education is an element of that following that leads to our transformation. Often churches define education as only Bible study, which, of course, is profoundly important. However, Christian education must encompass not only an understanding of the biblical text, but also of how that text, lived out in the body of Christ, encounters the world. This means church history, theology, and, yes, church polity. To work its best, congregational polity requires an articulate, engaged, theologically literate, spiritually committed membership.

A third element of successful congregational polity is honest communication. I continually hear Baptist young people ask the question "Why can't we all just get along?" They deplore dissension and conflict. Many want to hide their heads in the sand or run looking for a place where peace and harmony reign. Their attitude probably is representative of the average Baptist. I urge them to view conflict as an opportunity rather than as an obstacle. Jesus told us that we would see conflict and suffering. When we bring our individuality and struggles together in corporate life, there will be differences. In the heat of the moment, it may seem easier to sweep the conflict under the rug or abdicate the decision to a strong leader. However, it is not a spiritual high road to ignore the conflict or to "let the pastor decide." Both of these options deny the responsibilities that come with being a part of the body of Christ.

The key is not to eliminate conflict, but rather to deal with conflict in a healthy manner—not how to "smile and get along," but how to disagree with grace. Congregational polity functions best in an atmosphere of open dialogue. Church members should practice talking together about important issues that affect their faith. Dialogue can be accomplished in any number of ways. Business meetings, newsletters, roundtable discussions, and other methods of communication are crucial in the life of a Baptist church.

One congregation introduces important theological issues with dramatic presentations and invites the members to dialogue openly about the concepts raised. Some congregations have "family discussions" or "table talks" on Wednesday nights where the church can study difficult issues and discuss them. Unfortunately, church business meetings often become heated because these are the only avenues for open dialogue in the life of the faith family.

These discussions should not be free-for-alls, of course. They should be very intentional opportunities for civil discourse. Choosing a wise moderator is extremely important. Pastors usually should avoid this role, if possible. A church should adopt a code of conduct for its community discourse, emphasizing kindness, gentleness, respect, compassion, and thoughtfulness. The community should not tolerate sarcasm, slander, or cruelty when it meets together as the family of God. Being Christian does not mean that we cease thinking, talking, or even disagreeing; it means that we conduct ourselves in a manner worthy of the gospel of Christ.

We are learning about civil discourse, good order, and the unity of the body of Christ from our senior adults at our church. When the deacons' meeting ended that August day, the church membership met for a chat before the pastor came in view of a call. Everyone was invited to come, to listen, and to voice concerns. The fellowship hall was full. In spite of the difficult topic of "women in ministry," the dialogue was civil and, for the most part, gracious. After all of the speeches were made, an older gentleman stood up to "say his peace." He usually keeps us on our toes in business meetings, asking the troubling questions and generally placing his finger on the sore spots. So once again we held our breath, waiting for the storm. "Well, I don't know about a woman as a pastor," he said. "I may vote against her. I probably will vote against her. But, I tell you this, if the church votes for her, we all have to support her or she will never make it." Then he sat down.

With this simple selfless speech he eloquently exhibited a profound commitment to unity in the church. He remained true to his word. When the congregation voted to call the recommended candidate by an overwhelming majority, the gentleman remained a faithful member of the church. "Make my joy complete," Paul wrote to the Philippians, "be of the same mind, having the same love, being one in full accord and one of mind" (Philippians 2:2).

Congregational polity means that we cannot abdicate our personal responsibility before God to be concerned about, or to participate in, the life of the church. We must apply our whole heart and mind to the issues that face us. The freedom of the local church brings with it responsibility. We are the body of Christ. We are to show Christ to the world. The blessing and the curse of congregational polity is that the local church is only as powerful as the passion of its people, its vision only as far-reaching as the gaze of its members. Congregational freedom carries with it tremendous potential that balances on the radical notion that individual believers will be conformed to the image of Christ.

Notes

1. Nancy Ammerman, "Citizens/Baptists: Equal Souls, Voluntary Churches, Missionary Ambassadors," speech given at the Pruit Memorial Symposium, Baylor University, Friday, October 2, 2009. These quotations are from my personal notes.
2. See Stanley J. Grenz, *The Baptist Congregation: A Guide to Baptist Belief and Practice* (Valley Forge, PA: Judson Press, 1985), 54.
3. "First London Confession," in H. Leon McBeth, *A Sourcebook for Baptist Heritage* (Nashville: B&H Academic, 1990), 50.
4. Grenz, *The Baptist Congregation*, 54.
5. McBeth, *Sourcebook for Baptist Heritage*, 34.
6. Thomas Helwys, "The Mistery of Iniquity, 1612," in McBeth, *Sourcebook for Baptist Heritage*, 72.
7. Leonard Busher, "Religion's Peace, 1614," in McBeth, *Sourcebook for Baptist Heritage*, 73.
8. George W. Truett, *Baptists and Religious Liberty* (Dallas: Dallas Offset, 1981), 3.
9. Ibid.
10. Benjamin Griffith, "An Essay on the Power of an Association, 1749," in McBeth, *Sourcebook for Baptist Heritage*, 146.
11. McBeth, *Sourcebook for Baptist Heritage*, 44.
12. William G. McLoughlin, *New England Dissent 1630–1833: The Baptists and the Separation of Church and State*, vol. 1 (Cambridge: Harvard University Press, 1971), 53.
13. McLoughlin, 69.

CHAPTER 9

A SERMON ON THE BAPTIST DISTINCTIVE OF
Christian Calling

Prenatal Ordination

RALPH DOUGLAS WEST
Jeremiah 1:1-10

The call to the ministry is a curious thing. It is a mystery beyond any definition, and it comes from God on high to particular people in different ways, begetting various patterns of human response. One such example was exemplified in the life of G. Campbell Morgan, the famous British expositor, more than sixty of whose books are still in print, who from his earliest youth wanted to be a preacher. At that young age he would hold memorial services for dogs and cats, fishes and birds for other little children who gathered around to hear his animal funeral homilies. Driven to be a preacher, he appeared before a Methodist ordination council and preached a trial sermon, but the council turned him down flat. They advised Morgan to become a school teacher instead of a preacher. The melancholy Morgan sent his father a one-word telegram: "Rejected." It is said that his encouraging father sent back a telegram response: "Rejected on earth but selected in heaven." And by and by, Campbell Morgan showed the world he was called to preach through his tenacious pursuit of his ministerial vocation.

On the other hand, we have the example of Rev. Dr. Gardner Calvin Taylor. Taylor did *not* want to be a preacher. This very famous preacher wanted to be an attorney until an automobile wreck on a dark Louisiana road and an inquest in a courtroom thrust him into a ministry that he, at least initially, did not want.

There was a Morgan who wanted to be a preacher and initially could not. There was a Taylor who looked like he didn't want to be a preacher but ultimately couldn't avoid it. The call of God is a mystery. But the life and calling of the prophet Jeremiah demonstrates some sense of commonality about the call of God. How God called Jeremiah tells us several things about this divine initiation.

First and foremost, in that call of God there are *externals* for us all and *eternals* for us all. And the externals, like the eternals, may vary in the specifics but they're the same in the spirit.

The Externals of the Context

You read in the context of Jeremiah's call the externals of that call. He had an identity, a family, a locality, and a history. And for every one of us whom the Lord calls, God makes no mistake about our identity, our family, our locality, and our history.

We might see that the **identity** of Jeremiah was right there in his name: Jeremiah. Go to the exegetes, and some of them will tell you that his name means "Jehovah exalts." Go to others, and they will tell you that it means "Jehovah hurls down." Right there in his name is a cameo of his ministry. Here was a man whose identity was to be so exalted that he was able to glimpse the new covenant that Jesus referenced in the upper room at the Last Supper. Yet here also was someone who was "hurled down." Jeremiah was a man who had to be odd for God: Having to wear a loin cloth, having to go and bury it, and then going to dig it up and bring it back.

Those who experience the call of God on their life often encounter that same tension. The call of God is to have an identity that may have within it a tension, sometimes one of exaltation and sometimes one of being hurled down.

Jeremiah did not only have his identity, he also had his **family**. He was the son of Hilkiah. Some try to romanticize this Hilkiah and make him a figure who was active in the revival of Josiah. I would rather think not. The thing about Hilkiah was that he was a common, undistinguished, anonymous, unknown priest. The roots of Jeremiah were in anonymity, not notoriety. Have you ever noticed how God delights to reach down into that which has no precedence or pedigree, no priority and no purpose? In essence, God says, "I am going to reach into a nobody who's from nowhere, and I am going to make that nobody into somebody." And that is what God did with Jeremiah, and that is what God does still today.

Then look at his **locality**. Anathoth was a tiny little village whose location is uncertain today but perhaps may have been on a hill three miles northeast of Jerusalem. It was an isolated, unnoticed, nowhere kind of place. And yet God reached down to that place and essentially said, "I am going to choose a prophet for the nations from this little place that is from nowhere."

Jeremiah, then, not only had an identity, a family, and a locality, but he also had a **history**. And that is bracketed in the names of these mighty rulers that you read, three of the five of whom are named in the text. There was Josiah, who had that revival which seemed to outsiders to be so genuine, and yet Jeremiah would critique it as being merely external and formal. Then there was Johoakim, the vacillating king, and then there was Zedekiah the last pitiful king, willing but weak. They defined the history in which the ministry of Jeremiah took place.

You see, like Jeremiah, all of us are thrust down into our times— not only to bring a word about "was-ness" but a word that is given to bring "is-ness"—to get the word out of Jerusalem and get it into Houston or Vegas, LA or Chicago, Boston or Phoenix or wherever you are from, and to bring about the present power of a past event.

The Eternals of the Call

But if that is all you can say about Jeremiah, all you would have said is that Jeremiah was born, he lived, and he died. However, the thing that makes the difference is what you read in verse 2: "to whom the word of the LORD came." That *dabar Yahweh*, that charged unit, when it came out of the mouth of God, made everything different for Jeremiah. It was just incidental that in the externals of his context he had an identity, family, locality, and a history. The thing that lifted him up into the ages was that into that external came the eternal. The word of the Lord came. And that is what kept Jeremiah's epitaph from simply reading "born this year, died that year."

We don't know how the word of God came. We don't know if it came in a vision by day or in a dream by night. We don't know if it came when he was meditating out on the hills around Jerusalem. We don't know if it came in an audible voice. Whether the word came in the subjective or the objective, the significant thing is that the word of the Lord came. That arrested Jeremiah and claimed him, and everything else was changed because of that encounter.

Can you identify at all with this passage? I can. I can look at my own identity, my own family, my own locality, and my own history. And if that was all that was said about me, my life's epitaph would simply read, "He was born in July 1959 and died." But one day in July 1975, the word of the Lord came to me. Inside the common context of my identity, family, locality, and history, God reached down to a nobody from nowhere and called me to be his somebody. Something eternal came and brought to me a sense of significance. And that is what the call of God does.

You see, all of us share the common externals of life. It is the "giveness" of human existence. It is the confines of our life. But into the pedestrian externals of our life comes that eternal moment when God says, "I am calling you."

Somebody asked me once, "Did God call you in an audible voice?" I responded, "God called me a lot louder than that!" My life has led me to a lot of mysteries, but one thing is certain and that is the "word of the Lord came to me." That exceeds all of the other externals. And so I wonder, did that come to you?

If it comes at all, it comes at God's call, and that call is a *confrontation*, it is a *conversation*, and it is a *confirmation*.

A Confrontation

God is over against me. One of the biggest things you can learn in ministry is that the Lord is God and you are not. How does that confrontation come?

A Claim

First it comes as a **claim**: "Before I formed you in the womb I knew you." That word *yada*, which means "I knew you" also means "I claimed you." Do you understand what God is saying to Jeremiah? "No claim in your life is prior to my claim. Before you drew your first breath, when you were the soft viscera growing beneath the heart of your mother, I claimed you."

Life is a series of increasing claims. When you are little, Mom and Dad have a claim on you. You go to school, and the college has a claim on you. You get called to a church; the church has a claim on you. You get in the denomination, and it can really get a claim on you. Claim after claim, but understand this: no claim is prior to God's claim. One of the things that will sustain you in ministry is to remember that God confronted you back there and said: "My claim is prior to every other claim."

A Consecration

Along with that claim is the **consecration**: "Before you were born I *sanctified* you." That's a great Hebrew word, *kedosh*, meaning "something that is utterly set apart." The closest we might come to the Jewish understanding of this word would be our modern thinking about radioactivity. When the Hebrews thought about holiness or consecration, they thought about it the same way we think about radioactivity. Radioactivity can either bless or it can blast. If you drop it as a bomb, it blasts. Yet when used carefully by cancer doctors and nuclear scientists, radiation has the ability to bless—with a cure, with energy, with power. In the spiritual sense, God's *kedosh* is radioactive—powerful enough to bless or blast. And as one called and consecrated by God, if I touched you, we also might say that your life becomes spiritually radioactive with my presence.

Consecration is a kind of ordination. You know what kind of ordination Jeremiah had? He had "prenatal" ordination. Here God said, "I set you apart before you were even born." That is the difference between having to preach a message and having a message to preach. Jeremiah excoriated those pseudo-prophets in Jerusalem who ran when they had not been sent and who spoke when they had not been spoken to. I want you to understand that, like Jeremiah, I believe I was set apart prenatally. Do you have a sense of that in your life? There is an inescapability of what God called you to do.

A Consignment

When God confronts us, God claims us and consecrates us, but God also **consigns** us: "I ordained you as prophet to the nations." How strange that is. Here is an unknown, anonymous, teenage boy from a little village, and God seizes him and says to him, "Your ministry is not going to be to that little village; it is not just going to be to Jerusalem, Judah, or Benjamin. You are going to belong to the nations and to the ages." As the old saying goes, "The proof of the pudding is in the eating," because here in the twenty-first century, we read these same words in a nation that Jeremiah could have never imagined. Is God's word true?

Today, while you can't find a copy of the *Jerusalem Gazette* from 627 BCE, you can certainly find the book of Jeremiah. And in that book are recorded God's word to Jeremiah then and God's word later to me: "I am consigning you to the nations."

Many of you know that I teach seminary students; these are young people going into the ministry. I used to be amazed when I would hear them say, "I would like to settle here in Texas" or "I would like to go to the home mission field" or "I'm from the Midwest, so I'd really like to go back to the Midwest." Listen: that is not your consignment! When God calls, God consecrates and then God consigns. Your safety is in that divine consignment. And your risk is not being in God's consignment. I thought I was consigned in one direction and got reassigned in another direction. It is God's assignment. That is beyond my imagination or invention or manipulation or creation. The call of God is in a confrontation: the Lord claims you, consecrates you, and consigns you.

From Confrontation to Conversation

God is over against me as the Holy One. The Lord confronts me—but then the Lord converses with me. You read the Book of Jeremiah, and that is the big difference between the one true God and the idols. The idols don't have anything to say. But the Lord God addresses me by name and enters into a conversation with me.

Look at Jeremiah's part of that conversation: "Ah, Lord God." He pleads his inability: "I cannot speak." Then he pleads his inexperi-

ence: "I am a youth." The word he used here is one commonly used
for an infant or a boy. What Jeremiah was claiming here was that he
was barely on the edge of maturity. In all likelihood he was a teenager
when this word came. When he was confronted, he pleaded his
inability and his inexperience.

Paul Tillich said, "One who has never tried to flee God has never
encountered God." If you are totally at ease with the task of preaching; if when God called you, you said, "Well, God, I am the one you
want! Here is my résumé, and really, where have you been?"; if there
is nothing in this call that has caused you mixed emotions and utter
ambivalence—"Yes, God, but no"—then you probably haven't
understood the call of God.

Sometimes I still marvel at what an incredible thing this is—for a
mere mortal like me to claim that I am speaking for God. You would
have to have an ego complex that would make Napoleon look humble. As C. H. Spurgeon said in his lectures to his students, "If you can
do anything else, do it." There have been times when I have said,
"God, I would like to resign from this whole thing completely." But
guess what? God always says, "No!"

When confronted by God's call, most of us, like Jeremiah, want a
little more conversation with the Lord. "Are you sure about this,
God? I'm not much of a prize, Lord. I'm afraid. I'm ill-equipped. I'm
too young. I'm too old. This was never in the plan—was it?"

In Conversation Comes Confirmation

And in the course of that conversation, the Lord confirms the calling.
With our inability and our inexperience, how dare we stand to speak
for God? Only with divine confirmation. God confirms the call with
a promise of *direction*, an assurance of *deliverance*, and with a
demonstration of power.

Divine Direction

After Jeremiah gave his Moses-like demurring demand, the Lord got
back into the conversation. God said, "I am going to give you direction, I am going to direct your movement, and I am going to direct
your message."

"Do not say I am a youth," the Lord said to Jeremiah. Instead, God directed Jeremiah's movements: "You will go to all whom I send you to." And God directed Jeremiah's message: "Whatever I shall command you shall speak."

"I am going to direct your movements," the Lord tells us. "Your going will be in my sending. I am going to direct your message. And your speaking will be in my saying." When our going is God's sending and our speaking is God's saying, then (and only then) do we dare speak for the Lord.

I look in life's rearview mirror now and see the little pastorates I had in Dallas, Texas, and Brookshire, Texas, and the Heights area in Houston. Yes, Jeremiah was right. My going was in God's sending, and my speaking was in God's saying. Your security is not in your contract with the church or your package or your percentage or your credentials but in God's sending and God's saying.

Divine Deliverance

And then there is the assurance of divine deliverance. A person who has never preached cannot understand this, but God said to Jeremiah: "Do not be afraid of their faces." From the pulpit, I have seen some fearful faces, some angry faces, some mean faces! Don't be unnerved when you stand up in the presence of those who feel like they would be doing God a service if they could eliminate you. The essence of knowing God means knowing God's deliverance. The Lord is not only the God who put on the Exodus, but One who puts on one exodus after another! The key event that shaped the consciousness of Israel was the great Exodus: when the Lord reached into history to deliver God's people from slavery and oppression in Egypt. And the Lord wanted Jeremiah to know that he is still in the exodus business. "Don't be afraid of their faces; I am with you to deliver you," God said.

Jeremiah needed that assurance in his ministry. You see, they tried to get him. They even tried to cut up his book. You remember that cynical king with his pen knife? He cut up that scroll and threw it in the brazier in the floor of his winter palace. Not only did he try to destroy the man, but he also tried to destroy his message. And God gave it all back to Jeremiah. When God calls, God is in the business of deliverance. And that is your security.

You ever walk the floor at night? You ever fret over a business meeting? You ever have the members plotting to vote you out of the church? I wish I had some of that sleep back. It finally dawned on me that my only security was in the Lord. God proposes and God disposes. Blessed be the name of the Lord.

Divine Demonstration

We are frail, mortal, finite creatures. We are caught in the time-space continuum. We need a demonstration. And God knows our frame, that we are dust. So, God gives us a demonstration. Look at the demonstration for Jeremiah: "Then the Lord put out his hand and touched my mouth; and the Lord said to me, 'Now I have put my words in your mouth . . . .'"

I don't know if Jeremiah was out on a hill in Anathoth. I don't know if he was in the temple, meditating in that great edifice of Solomon, or if he was in a trance in the wilderness. And I don't know if there was an objective, empirical hand that came out of heaven, or if there was a subjective sense that he was touched by whatever happened. These things I do not know. Whatever it was, however, it was a demonstration that left no uncertainty that God had called Jeremiah. And Jeremiah never doubted it again.

I think this is something interesting to observe here. In this demonstration it was God who touched Jeremiah's mouth. It was not another prophet who touched his mouth. God did not call up Elijah and say, "Touch his mouth." That is to say, the Lord did not give a second-hand message. Indeed, Jeremiah would prophesy against those prophets who borrowed one another's words. That's a challenge to us today: If God has called you to speak the Word, then wrestle with that Word until God gives you the message *you* are meant to proclaim.

I recognize that there has been a time when we each have been tempted to design a "Saturday night special," when we might put something in the meditative microwave. And there have been times when I was thankful for the *Best Black Sermons*, or one of Donald Parsons's audio tapes or one of Jasper Williams's albums. But that had better be for inspiration and not mere emulation. You need not to let another prophet touch your lips.

Note also that Jeremiah did not touch his own lips. We live in a day of invented messages parading under the name of the gospel. But the real gospel is not something that is ours to invent. If we have grown weary of telling the old, old story, we have just grown too weary. You can certainly get a crowd by inventing a message, but the gospel is not an invented message. Jeremiah did not touch his own lips.

Nor did the congregation come and touch Jeremiah's lips with an imposed message. They did not come to him and say: "Here is the congregational committee on preaching. We are going to put our words in your mouth, and we have determined the program." The most miserable existence you can live as a preacher is if some other prophet touches your lips, or you have to touch your own lips and muster something *ex nihilo* (out of nothing) every Sunday. And if the congregation imposes a message on your lips, then no God has touched your lips. Instead, I tell you, get alone and get in silence with God, open the Word and stay there until God touches your lips!

In our Baptist tradition, we have a process by which the local church licenses and ordains, committees and councils confirm, and seminaries and CVs testify to our credentials. This process is part of the power and privilege of our ecclesiology. And yet that same tradition recognizes that our calling originates not with credentials or votes, with exegetical abilities or oratorical skills. Instead, the process only confirms what God has already done—in confrontation, in conversation, and in confirmation. Each one who experiences that call to ministry knows the element of authenticity found in getting alone with God. God's people perceive and recognize that authenticity alone—and in ordination, the community of believers affirms that this person has been with God and has been called by God.

From Confirmation to Commission

Now after the confrontation of the call, after the conversation, and after the confirmation, God gives his commission. Listen to the commission for Jeremiah: "I have set you over the nations." Remember, this is to a teenage boy. In essence, God was saying: "The scope of your ministry is going to be to Egypt and Assyria and the ages. And

Jeremiah, you are going to pull down and destroy before you build up and plant."

Not all of us are given a message that something good is going to happen. Jeremiah was not given good news either. His message was that something bad was going to happen. Now I tell you to brace yourself, for it is coming. The eternal content of our message in our own external contexts and in our own age is not our choice. For some, all the work seems to be planting and building up. There are others for whom the prophet's mantle is heavy, and the message is about tearing down and destroying. In the Hebrew here, God uses two metaphors—one agricultural and one architectural. The agricultural image was one of pulling up something by its roots. The architectural image was that of destroying a building. And only when that building is down can you rebuild; only when you have uprooted the tares can you plant good seed.

Strikingly different from these images was the metaphor of our Lord Jesus Christ in the Sermon on the Mount. There he said, "You are salt and you are light. You are going to be the salt that retards rot and prevents putrefaction and delays deterioration. And you are going to do that by executing a ministry that preserves. And then you will be the warm light that shows the way home."

Are these words all that different than the words prophesied by Jeremiah about One who was to come? In the new covenant passage of Jeremiah 31, the prophet saw God like we would see the mast of a ship, just tipping over the horizon. Jeremiah prophesied that there was a new covenant coming. But little did he know that the One bringing that new covenant would also be from a little town from nowhere, from an adoptive father and a mother who were nobodies; that the One to come would have a history too, that history of Augustus and Tiberius and Herod. The One to come would also be bigger than that history. And when that One came, there would be a tearing down. He would say, "Yes, you destroy this temple." But would there be a building up? Yes, for it would be raised up on the third day!

CHAPTER 10

A SERMON ON THE BAPTIST DISTINCTIVE OF THE
Autonomy of the Local Congregation

A Congregational Dream

DAVID E. WILHITE
Galatians 3:26-28

Theological Background: Autonomy

The Baptist distinctive known as the autonomy of the local congregation represents Baptists at their best and at their worst.

As for the best, Baptists have rightly asserted that the universal church is manifested only in local churches, or congregations. Moreover, they rightly argue that the first-century church did not exist as a hierarchical institution governed by bishops, synods, or popes. Instead, the first-century Christians were a loose band of diasporic people who gathered locally to confess Jesus Christ as Lord. Baptists rightly insist that from the first century through the twenty-first century the primary sphere of the Spirit's activity is in local congregations. Autonomous local congregations retain the freedom and agility to react to any new context. Autonomous local congregations exhibit the ability to incarnate into any culture, to manifest God's body to any people, and to answer God's call immediately in any situation. Baptists and other free-church congregationalists need not wait on the slow-moving red tape of bureaucratic institutions. Baptists can send William Carey to India without the British government's permission; they can send teams of volunteers to work and serve the day after a hurricane devastates a community; they can plant new churches wherever a witness is needed with or without a proper church building. For Baptists, the well-known children's ditty is easily changed:

> Here is the church, but where is the steeple?
> It matters not; the church *is* the people![1]

The autonomy of the local congregation is often where Baptists are at their best.

On the other hand, the autonomy of the local congregation is often where Baptists are at their worst. In 1845 most Baptists were associating in what was known as the Triennial Convention. This convention passed a motion that barred any slave owner from being a missionary. In response, autonomous Baptist congregations in the South broke from that convention and formed the Southern Baptist Convention, in which it was recognized that any autonomous local congregation could send anyone whom it felt led to send as a missionary, even if that person were a slave owner. Was this not autonomous congregationalism gone horribly wrong?

Let us look at this word *autonomy*. It comes from the Greek words *autos* ("self") and *nomos* ("law"). To be autonomous means to be self-governed, self-ruled. But wait. Is it not a problem for any Christian group to claim self-rule? We are supposed to be theonomous— God-ruled! How can we champion autonomy when it contradicts the notion of theonomy?

Perhaps we should think of this distinctive differently. Perhaps autonomous congregationalism is not so much a doctrine that we defend as it is sin that we confess. Are we autonomous, self-ruled, instead of theonomous, God-ruled? Too often, yes. But at least we are honest about it.

After all, what is the alternative? I am quite certain that episcopal and presbyterian forms of church governance are no more theonomous than congregationalism is. In fact, when I see denominational synods enforce integration, and the local church starts calling itself "Independent Presbyterian,"[2] or when I see local parishes withhold their offerings from their archdiocese in order to sway the magisterium,[3] I suspect that those congregations are much more autonomous than they are letting on. It seems that they were autonomous all along. I do not think that there is a true alternative to an autonomous local congregation, and I am sure that passing the buck up a hierarchy in no way ensures theonomy.

Does the autonomy of the local congregation risk problems? Yes. It is an unimaginable risk. But by risking autonomy we also risk theonomy. Are we always theonomous? No. Too often we are autonomous, but at least we are honest about it.

Personal Testimony: Local

I remember being twelve and asking my father (who was also my Baptist pastor) about the two churches that we just passed. On one side of the street the church sign just said "Baptist," but right across the street the other church's sign read "Missionary Baptist." "One is white," Dad answered, "and one is black." Somehow, this did not make any sense to me. But I realized there could be no further explanation.[4]

Years later, while I was in seminary and serving as a youth minister of a church in Birmingham, Alabama, I picked up the state Baptist paper and read an article by Samuel Pettagrue, the pastor of Sardis Missionary Baptist Church. His article was on the state of the church almost forty years after Martin Luther King Jr. famously stated that Sunday morning was the most segregated hour of the week. This, he explained, was not God's design for the church. That article sparked a conversation that led to my appointment under Rev. Pettagrue as the minister of Christian education at Sardis Missionary Baptist Church.

I tell you my story in hopes of changing the way we see "our" story, the story that we share.[5] The person in charge of ministerial placement where I went to seminary once told me that she could not send my résumé to black congregations, not because she was racist, but because she was a realist. Now, that same person, as standard procedure, sends students' résumés to congregations of all different ethnic demographics. When the Sardis Missionary Baptist Church trustees voted on my appointment, unbeknownst to me at the time (I was out of the room), one trustee stood up, declared, "We should hire one of our own," and stormed out of the meeting. I never heard that story until after announcing that I was leaving Sardis to pursue my doctorate. That same trustee had turned out to become my biggest advocate, and she had come to refer to me lovingly as "her little white preacher." I share my testimony because I know personally that the autonomy of the local congregation represents Baptists at their worst, but it also represents Baptists—all Baptists—at their best.

Sermonic Conclusion: Congregation

Galatians 3:26-28 reads, "For in Christ Jesus you are all children of God through faith. As many of you as were baptized into Christ have clothed yourselves with Christ. There is no longer Jew or Greek, there is no longer slave or free, there is no longer male and female; for all of you are one in Christ Jesus."

The Problem

The apostle Paul did not begin this letter with such friendly tones. In fact, he comes across as quite harsh in his comments to the Galatian Christians. In 1:6 he expresses astonishment at them for "deserting" the faith. That is a serious charge, but it pales in comparison to what he says in 1:8-9, when he breathes threats of them being "accursed" (KJV) and "eternally condemned" (NIV). The third chapter of the letter opens with the apostle Paul blasting them as "foolish Galatians" and saying that they are "bewitched." It gets just plain ugly in 5:12, when he expressed his wish that some of them would "castrate themselves." That is no way to talk on a Sunday morning, Paul! What is going on here to make Paul so upset?

The first clue comes in 1:2. Paul addresses this letter to the "churches" of Galatia. In no other letter does Paul address "churches," plural. In this period, Christians did not meet in church buildings; they met from house to house. It would be appropriate to call each of these home gatherings a "church" and to refer to many of these various home gatherings as "churches," plural. But Paul is very careful never to do that in opening his letters;[6] he always begins by addressing the "church," singular: "Paul, an apostle of Christ . . . to the church of God that is in Corinth" (1 Corinthians 1:1). We know that there would have been several churches in Corinth, with no way for all of the believers in Corinth to have met in one house, but Paul still addresses them as "the church of God in Corinth." The Bible makes it 100 percent clear that there is only one church, one body, one faith, one Lord (see Ephesians 4:4-5). While it is appropriate to refer to an individual congregation as a "church," ultimately it only represents *the* church. So when Paul writes to Christians in a certain city or region, he emphasizes that they are *the* church in their city, they are *the* church in Corinth, they are *the* church in Thessalonica (thus, *the* church in Birmingham, *the* church in Waco). He allows no room for division in the body. But here in Galatians he addresses the letter to the "churches" of Galatia.

The next clue comes from Galatians 2. Paul made it abundantly clear in 1:11 that he received his gospel directly from Christ, but now he stops to point out how his teachings lined up with the teaching of all the other apostles. He draws attention to this beginning in 2:1: when he went up to Jerusalem, where the Jews were, he took Barnabas, a Jew, and he also took Titus, a non-Jew, and they talked about how the gospel has been preached to the Gentiles. Clearly, there was no problem. This was the clear teaching of Christ for his church as handed down through all of the apostles.

But he says in 2:11, the problem started in Antioch. Paul and his buddies were doing fine; even Peter came up to visit, and there was no problem. But then, when some of the other Jewish believers came up from Jerusalem, the trouble began. It appears that Peter and the others began segregating themselves from the Gentile Christians. Even Barnabas joined this disjoining, to the point that he and Peter would not even "break bread" with the Gentiles. When Paul saw this, he was outraged.[7] The church of God at Antioch was now divided along racial lines: Jews and Gentiles. The problem at Antioch was segregation. And now this problem had infected the Christians in Galatia.[8] In fact, this might be why Paul addresses this letter to the "churches" of Galatia. It seems that entire congregations were meeting based on ethnicity. You might have heard it said in Galatia that "Sunday morning was the most segregated hour of the week." And for Paul, this is absolutely unacceptable, because no excuse is a good excuse for segregating the body of Christ.

The Solution

The most fundamental translation of the Greek word for "church," *ekklēsia*, is "congregation," a gathering.[9] The very definition of "church" as congregation is antithetical to segregation. There is no reason under any circumstances why the body of Christ should be segregated along racial, economic, or social lines.

I am as concerned as anyone about seeing integration in our society. But what this world needs is not integration but congregation. But we will never have integration in our society if we do not have congregation in our churches. Why would we have integration on Monday when we do not have congregation on Sunday? I believe in fighting for justice in this world, but I also believe that the church must take the lead in this fight. It was the church that brought about desegregation in 1960s, not the world. (It just so happened that, historically, it was mostly the black church, but it was the church.) But now, the church has fallen asleep. The church should not sit idly by while the world tries to move toward integration. The church must arise and preach the gospel of congregation and the gospel of reconciliation (see 2 Corinthians 5:18-19). The fight for justice does not begin on the steps of the capitol building; it begins at the altar of your church.

This is why Paul was so upset. The Christians in Galatia were segregated, and Paul knew no excuse is a good excuse for segregating the body of Christ.

But the Galatians were making excuses. In fact, the excuse that they give for their segregation is a "biblical" excuse: the Jews were saying that the Bible forbade them from worshiping with the uncircumcised Gentiles. So, Paul has to deal with their excuse. Now, I believe that today Baptists understand that "works of the law" (Galatians 3:2) will not save us. We understand that we are "justified by faith" (Galatians 3:24). Anyone who expects to get into heaven by "being good" is sadly mistaken. Galatians makes it perfectly clear that it is only by placing your faith in the risen Savior, Jesus Christ, that you will be saved.

So, as the people of God, we have gotten past the excuse of the Christians in Galatia. However, is it not sad that Christians are still dividing down racial lines today? Is it not sad that Christians are still making excuses for segregation in the church? "Well, none of them live in our neighborhood." Your neighborhood? Most of you do not go to church in your neighborhood! Most of our churches are in regions that are less than 60 percent white, and yet so many of them are 100 percent homogenous.

What is worse is that we are even making "biblical" excuses. People will say, "The Bible says, 'Do not be unequally yoked.'" Have you heard that one? I have even heard, "Well, Paul and Barnabas had a church split. Church splits are biblical!"

One woman said to me, "They just don't worship the way I do." I wanted to reply, "I'm sure they're thankful." But please, "They don't worship the way I do"? Neither did Jesus!

"Well, we just have our own way of doing things. It's society. It's tradition. People just won't change." Excuses, excuses, excuses. God's word tells us that no excuse is a good excuse for segregating the body of Christ by race, gender, or income.

The Obligations of a Congregation

Looking back at Galatians 3, we observe three important points about a congregation.

Galatians 3:26: "In Christ Jesus you are all children of God through faith."[10] This is good news! Because of what Jesus Christ, the Son of God, did for us two thousand years ago, we are now children of God. We can now call God "Our Father." We now have an inheritance waiting for us. We have been adopted into the royal line of the King of kings and Lord of lords. And as great as all of this is, the emphasis in 3:26 is that "all" are children of God. Not just you Jewish Christians, not just you Gentile Christians, not just you white Christians, not just you black Christians, not just you Hispanic Christians, not just you Asian Christians, but *all* of you are sons and daughters of God.

In 2008 Frank Pollard, a former professor at Truett Seminary, passed away. Betty Talbert shared one memory of when Frank was a pastor and he had been confronted by deacons who did not want to accept black people as members of the church.

> Frank told the deacons, "You fellows are wealthy and powerful, so maybe you can say no to the poor and black, but I had seven broth-

ers and grew up in a one-room house. I have heard my brothers ask
my daddy to give me away because I took food that they needed.
My daddy said that baby Frank was his son like they were his sons,
and that there would always be a place for Frank in his house."

Frank then said to the deacons, "My father did not turn me out
of his house, though many asked him to, and I cannot turn away
anyone who asks to enter my heavenly Father's house." The deacons changed their policy.

The first obligation of a congregation is to recognize our family unit.
I love my sister, Donna, and we have always been close. I am not
going to stop having fellowship with my sister because she likes more
or less excited forms of worship than I do. I am not going to stop seeing my sister because she makes more or less money than I do. I am
not going to stop loving my sister for any reason. We are a family, and
although families sometimes fight, they should never be divided
because of differences in pigmentation, employment, or culture. And
sisters and brothers, we are the family of God, and no excuse is a
good excuse for segregating the family of God.

Look at the next verse, Galatians 3:27. Paul tells us that we have
"clothed" ourselves with Christ. Again, there is the emphasis that all
of us have done this. All who have been baptized into Christ have
been clothed with Christ. First, in order to put on Christ, you have to
take off sin. Before you put on the new self, you must take off the old
self. Before you can have the fruit of the Spirit mentioned in Galatians
5:22-23, you must reject "acts of the sinful nature" discussed in Galatians 5:19-21. There are some who think that we should just be tol-
erant and accepting of everyone, whether adulterous deacons or
bisexual bishops. But the clear teaching of Scripture requires that in
order to be accepted into this loving and unified body of believers,
you must repent. The umbrella of Christian unity does not cover
those who willingly live a life of sin. You must "put on Christ."

To "clothe yourself with Christ" is the image of a new uniform.
When you are baptized in front of witnesses for all the world to see,
you have declared whose side you are on. You have put on the uniform of Christ Jesus himself, as symbolized in the white robes of the
early Christians.

In 2008 Baptists from all denominations in North America were invited to the Celebration of a New Baptist Covenant in Atlanta. For the three days prior to that meeting the four historic black Baptist denominations met jointly. Truett Seminary sent me to set up a recruiting booth during the black Baptist meetings. Ours was the only seminary represented, and I was one of the few white persons in the exhibit hall. One man asked me pointedly, "Who are you folks at Truett? Are you Southern Baptists?" I was unsure what answer he wanted to hear. I tried to explain how we would be more aligned with the Cooperative Baptist Fellowship in those terms, but that we are formally aligned with the Baptist General Convention of Texas, and more importantly how we accept and train Baptists from all denominations. He responded, "Good! Because we know that the Southern Baptists were founded so that they could own slaves, and we know that Southern Baptists aren't here at this [New Baptist Covenant] meeting because they're racists, and we're glad you're here!" Now, that is not entirely fair (it is not entirely unfair either), but we should ask: Cannot Baptists from all ethnicities work together? And since we can work together, can we not worship together? I am not suggesting that we all become color-blind. Our cultural and ethnic heritage is important and should not be overlooked. I am suggesting, however, that those differences are secondary to the fact that we have all been baptized into Christ, and we all wear the same uniform.

Do you think that U.S. soldiers fighting in Afghanistan care about the color of the soldiers fighting alongside them? No way! If you are wearing the same uniform that I am wearing, I am glad that you are here. Christians, we are the army of God, and all who have Christ in them are our allies. We must learn to look for the inner clothing of Christ, not for the outer garments of culture and class. When we see our brothers and sisters, we should not care so much about what is under their robe; we should care about who is in their heart.

Finally, in Galatians 3:28 Paul completely spells out God's vision for Christ's church: "There is neither Jew nor Greek, slave nor free, male nor female, for you are all one in Christ Jesus" (NIV). Once again, notice the emphasis. How many of you are one in Christ? "All."

Notice Paul's apophatic ecclesiology—that is, Paul's definition of the church by clarifying what the church is *not*. It is not a gathering around culture, class, gender, or any other social stratification; those descriptors are all cast out into the "neither" regions. For the record, a youth group is not a church. Certainly it is churchlike; the youth group meeting may do churchly things, but it is not church. The criteria that define the youth group are being gathered in the name of Christ and the members being of a certain age. For the record, a women's Bible study is not church. Again, it is churchlike; the women's Bible study meeting involves churchly things, but it is not church. The criteria that define a women's Bible study are being gathered in the name of Christ and the members being of a certain gender. The problem with a segregated local church is not that it is autonomous; the problem is that it is not church!

Paul has now made this idea of church perfectly clear: when God places a church in Galatia, he expects it to be made up of Galatians, whether they are Jewish Galatians or Greek Galatians, black Galatians or white Galatians, rich Galatians or poor Galatians, contemporary-worship Galatians or traditional-worship Galatians. God's plan is simply to have a congregation of Christian Galatians, and they are all to be "one in Christ Jesus." And no excuse is a good excuse for segregating the body of Christ.

Conclusion

Before I conclude, I want to say that I am not here to judge. The segregation on Sunday morning is not your fault, and it is not your church's fault. Moreover, we should not go pointing fingers at our parents' generation.

I am not here to judge; I am here to offer a word of encouragement. The Bible tells us that segregation in the church is completely against the will of God. And I believe that racial reconciliation can happen.

I believe that a day will come when there is racial reconciliation in America, and that it will come through the church. I believe that a day will come when there are no more black churches and white churches. There will be no Hispanic churches or Asian churches. There will be no rich churches or poor churches. There will only be Christian churches.

I know that this sounds idealistic, maybe even unrealistic. Where else will black Christians be able to express themselves in their own culture as they worship? Where else will Spanish-speaking or Korean-speaking Christians be able to freely confess their faith? I do not have all the answers, but I know that we cannot give up because of excuses. I do not know what tomorrow holds, but I know who holds tomorrow.

So, let me paraphrase the words of one wise leader of our past.[11]

I am not unmindful that some of you come from and belong to long-standing traditions. Some of you are confined in what you can do because of cell walls of narrow-mindedness. Some of you have come from situations where your quest for reconciliation left you wearied from standing against the storms of pessimism and staggered by the winds of Christian hypocrisy. You have been conditioned to think that the situation is hopeless. Continue to work with the faith that such struggles are redemptive.

We must continue in our congregation; we must continue in the churches of Galatia, continue in the segregated and divided body of Christ, knowing that somehow this situation can and will be changed. Let us not wallow in the valley of despair.

I say to you today, my sisters and brothers, that in spite of the difficulties and frustrations of the moment, we, as Christians, still have a dream—a *congregational* dream. We have a dream that one day the body of Christ will rise up and live out the true meaning of its commission: to preach the gospel to all nations.

We have a dream that one day in the pews of any Southern church the children of former slaves and the children of former slave owners will be able to sit down together in the bonds of brotherhood.

We have a dream that one day even the most racist congregations, churches of hate and oppression, will be transformed into communities of love and acceptance.

We have a dream that our children's church membership will be determined not by the color of their skin but by the Christ-clothes that they have put on.

We still have a dream today.

We have a dream that one day every valley shall be exalted, and every mountain and hill made low; the crooked places shall be made straight, and the rough places made plain; and the glory of the Lord shall be revealed, and all flesh shall see it together.

This is our hope. This is the faith with which we go out to serve. With this faith we will see drawn out of the chaos of Babel a fellowship of Pentecost. With this faith we will be able to transform the jangling discords of our churches into a beautiful symphony. With this faith we will be able to work together, pray together, be persecuted together, and stand up for the gospel together, knowing that we will be one in Christ.

This will be the day when all of God's children will be able to say with a new meaning, "There *is* neither Jew nor Greek, there *is* neither slave nor free, there *is* neither male nor female, for you *are* all one in Christ Jesus."

Notes

1. While this pitiful excuse for poetry is my own, I am indebted to the much more articulate and insightful work of Miroslav Volf, *After Our Likeness: The Church as the Image of the Trinity* (Grand Rapids: Eerdmans, 1998), whose opening line is "We are the people!" which is used to insist "We are the church!"

2. See R. Milton Winter, "Division and Reunion in the Presbyterian Church, U.S.: A Mississippi Retrospective," *Journal of Presbyterian History* 78, no. 1 (2000): 67–86.

3. Fox Butterfield, "Boston Archdiocese, Hurting Financially, Warns of Layoffs," *New York Times*, June 18, 2003.

4. This is the majority culture's luxury of "blinders" talked about in Spencer Perkins and Chris Rice, *More Than Equals: Racial Healing for the Sake of the Gospel*, rev. ed. (Downers Grove, IL: InterVarsity Press, 2000), 70–84.

5. See James Wm. McClendon Jr., *Biography as Theology: How Life Stories Can Remake Today's Theology* (Philadelphia: Trinity Press International, 1990).

6. Or elsewhere, for that matter. Paul uses "churches" only when explicitly differentiating ethnically divided congregations (see Romans 16:4-16; 1 Corinthians 7:17-20; 16:1-19; 1 Thessalonians 2:14; and probably 2 Thessalonians 1:4), the exceptions being 1 Corinthians 11:16-22; 2 Corinthians 8–12, where "churches" is used for congregations divided by class, and in reference to the ecclesial divisions mentioned in 1 Corinthians 14:33-35 having to do with gender. Similarly,

compare Luke's (Pauline) usage of "church" in the singular, including references to multiple congregations in various regions (Acts 9:31; 20:17), whereas in Acts 15:41; 16:5 reference is made to the "churches" being strengthened by the ruling of the Jerusalem council—that is, ethnically segregated congregations that receive the mandate to be reconciled into one church.

7. For a pastorally sensitive and helpful commentary on this exchange, see Augustine's commentary on this letter (*Augustine's Commentary on Galatians*, trans. and ed. Eric Plumer, Oxford Early Christian Studies [Oxford: Oxford University Press, 2003]).

8. The ethnic tensions between Jewish and Hellenistic believers in Paul's letters have largely been eclipsed by Westerners' myopic focus on "religious" or "doctrinal" issues, as if such matters could be separated from sociohistorical dynamics. For a postcolonial reading that finds ethnic tension in this work in particular, see Allan Boesak, *Walking on Thorns: The Call to Christian Obedience* (Grand Rapids: Eerdmans, 1984). Also, the "new perspective" on Paul understands the motif in Galatians to be that of "resisting practices used to reinforce a narrow ethnic exclusivity" (Markus Bockmuehl, "Peter between Jesus and Paul," in *Jesus and Paul Reconnected: Fresh Pathways into an Old Debate*, ed. Todd D. Still [Grand Rapids: Eerdmans, 2007], 71).

9. For my fuller explication of this issue, see Matt Jenson and David Wilhite, *The Doctrine of the Church: A Guide for the Perplexed* (Edinburgh: T & T Clark, 2010).

10. The exegetical issues of Galatians are numerous, and the standard commentaries may be consulted. For the recent debates around this particular issue, I recommend David Stubbs, "The Shape of Soteriology and the *pistis Christou* Debate," *Scottish Journal of Theology* 61, no. 2 (2008): 137–57.

11. Adapted from Martin Luther King Jr., "I Have a Dream" speech, delivered at the Lincoln Memorial in Washington, DC, on August 28, 1963. King's "Letter from a Birmingham Jail" has also significantly influenced my thinking about the risks of autonomous congregationalism.

SECTION FOUR
The Ordinances

Baptism and
The Lord's Supper

Baptists believe that two God-ordained ordinances are found in Scripture. However, this general notion of baptism and the Lord's Supper (which Baptists often also call "Communion") as the two special rites of the church is shared by most Protestant Christian traditions, and it originated from the theologians of the Reformation. In his Reformation treatise, "The Pagan Servitude of the Church," Martin Luther defined a sacrament as a promise of Christ accompanied by a sign.[1] From this understanding, he posited that five of the traditional seven sacraments of the Western church did not meet the criteria to be sacramental (i.e., conveying a promise of God and associated with a physical symbol) and thus were not to be recognized by the new Protestant church in Germany. Though often changing Luther's terminology, Baptists, like most other Protestants, subsequently retained baptism and the Lord's Supper as the two ordinances of the church. While a number of early English Baptists maintained the term *sacrament*,[2] most Baptists in the United States ultimately came to prefer the term *ordinance* so as to convey these rites as the ceremonies "specifically committed to the church for perpetual observance,"[3] performed in obedience to Christ, and so as to avoid intimating that these signs actually became the means of God's grace. Nevertheless, Baptists have asserted that the ordinances powerfully represent God's inward spiritual work through the symbols of water and of bread and cup.

Baptism

Unquestionably, believer's baptism is the central doctrine or practice by which Baptists historically are most identified. Baptists were so well known by this practice that the label "Baptist" originally was a pejorative term used by outsiders to identify those who held to baptizing only those who had already been converted. From the outset of the movement, then, the theology and the practice of believer's baptism were a hallmark of the Baptist witness. From their founding, Baptists eschewed the practice of infant baptism, seeing water baptism instead as the faithful response of the genuine believer to God's grace and as best replicating the apostolic practice. Baptists rejected the interpretation that infant baptism was a New Testament replacement for circumcision and instead argued that God was in the business of circumcising the heart through faith. Since faith was understood as a personal appropriation contingent upon each person's cognitive and heartfelt acceptance of God's grace, Baptists insisted that only those who were mature enough to apprehend Christ's work on Calvary and genuinely confess Jesus as Lord were acceptable candidates for the ordinance. Baptism became then for Baptists a public profession of faith of what God had already worked inwardly in redeeming the individual through Christ. Thus, as noted in the section on ecclesiology, baptism became the prerequisite for church membership of the local congregation and the gateway into the visible church of the saints of God.

Like most Anabaptists before them, the earliest Baptists baptized by pouring water. However, Particular Baptists in the 1640s recovered the ancient church practice of immersion and insisted on its sole use. General Baptists soon followed in this practice, so that by the 1660s all Baptists became known not only for their insistence upon baptizing only mature Christian believers, but also for the form of baptism of complete immersion for all candidates.[4] This form of baptism became the exclusive practice not only because Baptists understood the Greek word *baptizō*, used repeatedly in the New Testament, to mean "immerse" and thus saw themselves as strictly following the scriptural injunction, but also because the act of plunging a baptizand beneath the waters and raising him or her up again best replicated the apostle Paul's description of the rite in Romans 6:3-5:

> Do you not know that all of us who have been baptized into Christ Jesus were baptized into his death? Therefore we have been buried with him by baptism into death, so that, just as Christ was raised from the dead by the glory of the Father, so we too might walk in newness of life. For if we have been united with him in a death like his, we will certainly be united with him in a resurrection like his.

Thus, as Brian Brewer points out in his sermon on this topic (see chapter 11), baptism serves as a symbolic rehearsal not only of Christ's own death and resurrection, but also of the death of the old sinner and the rebirth and promised resurrection of the new person that each baptizand has become in Christ. The physical element of water represents the spiritual reality of this new birth (cf. John 3:5) and serves as part and parcel of each new believer's confession of and identity with Christ Jesus.

Baptists repudiated the practice of infant baptism for several reasons, among them that the Scriptures never specifically mention the baptism of the very young and that the Great Commission (Matthew 28:19-20) implies a proper order. In *A Small Treatise of Baptisme, or Dipping* (1641), Baptist leader Edward Barber explained,

> 1. They onely are to be dipped that are made Disciples by teaching, Matth. 28.19. Infants cannot be made Disciples by teaching, thefore [*sic*] Infants are not to be dipt. . . .
>
> 3. Againe, if the command of Christ our Savior for making disciples by teaching before they are dipt, . . . then it ought to bee performed and observed in the Church of Christ for ever.
>
> The Major is true, ... Therefore persons upon the manifestation of Repentance and faith onely are to be dipped.[5]

The teaching of the church is the first act of making disciples, Baptists claim. Upon apprehension of the faith and confession of sin, new Christians are then ready for baptism and entrance into the church of fellow Christian witnesses. The act of baptism comes as public testimony of one's newly found faith, and the burial in and raising from water serves as a powerful reminder of the death to the old person and the resurrection of the new, both for the baptizand and for all the gathered, faithful witnesses.

The Lord's Supper

Like the ordinance of baptism, the Lord's Supper traditionally has been understood by Baptists as a powerfully symbolic observance carried out in obedience to the command of Jesus in the context of corporate worship. Although the Lord's Supper received less attention in the early writings of Baptists than did baptism, its theology and practice are important in the life of Baptist congregations. The Philadelphia Confession of Faith (1689) notes,

> The Lord's Supper of the Lord Jesus Christ was instituted by him the same night wherein he was betrayed, to be observed in his churches

unto the end of the world, for the perpetual remembrance, and showing forth the sacrifice of himself in his death, confirmation of the faith of believers in all the benefits thereof, their spiritual nourishment and growth in him, their further engagement in and to all duties which they owe unto him, and to be a bond and pledge of their communion with him and with each other.[6]

This important ordinance rehearses the meal that Jesus shared with his disciples in the upper room, reminding the gathered faithful today that each Christian still numbers among Jesus' disciples. Figuratively and spiritually, then, each Christian was sitting with Jesus, and each hears again the words of institution as if said by Christ, in a ceremony now reenacted in memorial. Baptists may have acquired this understanding originally from the Swiss reformer Ulrich Zwingli and from the sixteenth-century Anabaptists who highlighted the apostle Paul's account of the words of Jesus, who said, "Do this . . . in remembrance of me" (1 Corinthians 11:25). Baptists believe that by partaking of the elements of bread and the cup, Christians are powerfully reminded of Christ's sacrifice in giving his body and pouring out his blood for the world's sake. At the same time, Baptists believe that no new sacrifice is made during the rite, for Christ's work on Calvary was sufficient for the salvation of all believers (cf. Hebrews 9:23-28; 10:11-18). Nevertheless, as the Philadelphia Confession states, the Lord's Supper takes on a spiritual purpose in binding the Christian once again not only to Christ and the promises and privileges of his fellowship, but also to the gathered community of faith and its ministry of the priesthood of all believers. While each new Christian entered into such privileges and responsibilities through baptism, the Lord's Supper serves as a means of regular renewal of that baptismal confession and initial intention to serve Christ and his church. Baptism then serves as a once-for-all-time event for each person to proclaim the faith, while the Lord's Supper is practiced repeatedly as an ordinance that sustains and renews this faith. Additionally, as Todd Still points out in his sermon on the Lord's Supper to follow, Communion serves as a continual corporate confession of Christ's sacrificial death for the sake of all who believe in him.

However, this powerful ceremony is not merely a memorial; it does not look only to past events, but instead possesses within it promises for the present and the future. Norman Maring and Winthrop Hudson explain,

> As visible symbols that reinforce the gospel preached in words, [the elements of the Lord's Supper] remind Christians of the incarnation, of which the high points were death, burial, resurrection, and exaltation. These events signify God's deliverance of humanity from sin, and they recall to the church that Christ is the reason for their existence. In looking back to the origins from which Christians have sprung, they remember that Christ is still their living Lord. They are encouraged to remember what God has done, in order to be more vividly aware of what God continues to do and has promised yet to do. . . . The remembrance of what God has done is thus a preparatory step to a fresh encounter with the living God, who is in their midst working out the divine purposes in and through them.[7]

Thus, Christians are to look back through the ordinance to recall Jesus Christ's accomplished work so as to be encouraged that he is continuing to bring this good work to completion. Just as humans physically need daily bread for survival, so too do they require the spiritual replenishment of Christ for continued strength. The Lord's Supper powerfully reminds Christians that the one who redeemed them will sustain them presently and will glorify them in the time to come. Therefore, this symbolic meal of renewal is both recollection and anticipation: "For as often as you eat this bread and drink the cup, you proclaim the Lord's death until he comes" (1 Corinthians 11:26).

Notes

1. See Martin Luther, "The Pagan Servitude of the Church," in *Martin Luther: Selections from His Writings*, ed. John Dillenberger (New York: Anchor Books, 1962), 279, 357.
2. See Brian C. Brewer, "Signs of the Covenant: The Development of Sacramental Thought in Baptist Circles," *Perspectives in Religious Studies* 36, no. 4 (2009): 407–20.
3. Everett C. Goodwin, *The New Hiscox Guide for Baptist Churches* (Valley Forge, PA: Judson Press, 1995), 129.
4. H. Leon McBeth, *The Baptist Heritage: Four Centuries of Baptist Witness* (Nashville: B&H Academic, 1987), 44–45.

5. Cited in H. Leon McBeth, *A Sourcebook for Baptist Heritage* (Nashville: B&H Academic, 1990), 42.
6. Philadelphia Baptist Association, *The Philadelphia Confession of Faith, with Catechism* (Grand Rapids: Associated Publishers and Authors, n.d.), 53.
7. Norman H. Maring and Winthrop S. Hudson, *A Baptist Manual of Polity and Practice*, rev. ed. (Valley Forge, PA: Judson Press, 1991), 163.

Action Steps for the Reader

1. For further reading on baptism and the Lord's Supper:

Beasley-Murray, G. R. *Baptism in the New Testament*. Grand Rapids: Eerdmans, 1962.

Johnson, Maxwell E. *The Rites of Christian Initiation: Their Evolution and Interpretation*. Collegeville, MN: Liturgical Press, 2007.

Moore, Russell D., et al. *Understanding Four Views on the Lord's Supper*. Grand Rapids: Zondervan, 2007.

Shurden, Walter B., ed. *Proclaiming the Baptist Vision: Baptism and the Lord's Supper*. Macon, GA: Smyth & Helwys, 1999.

Tyler, John R. *Baptism: We've Got It Right . . . and Wrong; What Baptists Must Keep, What We Must Change, and Why*. Macon, GA: Smyth & Helwys, 2002.

White, James F. *The Sacraments in Protestant Practice and Faith*. Nashville: Abingdon, 1999.

Witherington, Ben, III. *Making a Meal of It: Rethinking the Theology of the Lord's Supper*. Waco, TX: Baylor University Press, 2008.

Zwingli, Ulrich. "On True and False Religion." In *Zwingli: Commentary on True and False Religion*, ed. Samuel Macauley Jackson and Clarence Nevin Heller, 212–15. Durham, NC: Labyrinth Press, 1981.

2. Biblical texts for preaching and topical Bible study:

Baptism: Matthew 3:13-17; 28:19-20; Mark 1:9-11; Luke 3:21-22; John 1:29-34 (the baptism of Jesus); 3:5; Acts 2:38; 8:15-17, 36-38; 10:48; Romans 6:3-5; 1 Corinthians 1:13; 12:13.

The Lord's Supper: Exodus 12:6-8,24-27; Mark 14:22-26; Acts 2:42,46; 1 Corinthians 10:16-17,21; 11:23-29.

3. Ideas for worship:

Incorporate a new tradition of wrapping each newly baptized member in a white towel upon exiting the baptismal waters. Explain that such a tradition both replicates ancient Christian practice and represents the purity of the "new person" in Christ Jesus.

Before sharing the Lord's Supper, the minister may ask the members of the congregation to renew their baptismal confession, "Jesus is Lord," and any other customs or promises unique to your church's baptismal service. This will help the congregation tie the two ordinances together more tightly.

As the congregation prepares for the Lord's Supper or during the service of the meal, read the various passages listed at the bottom of page 129 regarding the Lord's Supper. It may be especially helpful to hear the Passover account from Exodus 12 to grasp better the Judeo-Christian understanding of remembrance as past, present, and future.

4. Opportunities for service:

Consider having a baptismal service outdoors in a public space, where safe and appropriate. This practice replicates the original Baptist understanding of baptism as a witness to the world as well as the church of one's confession of faith in Jesus Christ.

Conduct an outdoor Easter sunrise service that concludes with sharing Communion, with baskets of wafers and grapes representing the elements of bread and the cup.

CHAPTER 11

A SERMON ON THE BAPTIST DISTINCTIVE OF
Believer's Baptism

Down in the River to Pray

BRIAN C. BREWER

Matthew 28:19-20; Romans 6:1-8

Although this collection of sermons is on the theme of what we call "Baptist Distinctives," it is difficult to pinpoint any one distinctive belief or practice that Baptists own all to themselves. However, Baptists have contributed in so many areas of the Christian life, from the call for religious liberty for every individual to the understanding of congregational autonomy. Nevertheless, when boiled down to the very basics, probably the most visibly distinctive thing about Baptists, historically, is the way they baptize. Their very name comes from this practice. While our theological ancestors preferred to call themselves simply "the Church," or "the Church of Christ," or "Brethren," or "Baptized Churches,"[1] others pejoratively referred to them as those "rebaptizers" or "baptists" because they emphasized baptism so strongly, and so the name eventually stuck. And Baptist historians have argued that early English Baptists "defended [their baptismal practices] against Anglicans and Puritans, who wanted to baptize differently, and against Quakers, who didn't want to baptize at all."[2]

But over the course of time, Baptists may have forgotten why their tradition has made such a big deal about this ceremony. And here Baptists have always walked a fine line. We say that the baptismal waters do not save us, that God alone does that. There is nothing miraculous about the baptismal water, but only about the internal work of the Holy Spirit. Lost in all the nuanced discussion about the

rite is a fundamental question: why has water baptism been so important to Baptists? This was a question that Baptists were constantly
trying to answer while other Christians seemed to diminish the significance of the practice. As Peter Cartwright, a nineteenth-century
Methodist circuit rider, once quipped, "Baptists make so much ado
about baptism by immersion that the uninformed would suppose
that heaven was an island and the only way to get there was by swim-
ming or diving."[3]

So what is the big deal about baptism? Although Baptists do not
believe that baptism saves us, they do believe that it is inextricably
tied to our faith. We need to look no further than the New Testament
to find evidence of its importance.

First, we find John the Baptist baptizing his followers in the Jordan River when Jesus encounters him (Matthew 3:13-17). Jesus asks
to be baptized by John, too. What is interesting about this is that baptism was not necessarily a novel thing to those Jews in the first century. For some time many Jews used the *mikveh* (ritual bath) to
immerse things and people to cleanse them from their sinful influ-
ences. And the Essenes actually washed themselves daily in pools so
that they might be cleansed from sin. So here is Jesus, though not a
sinner himself, identifying with the sinfulness of humanity at the outset of his earthly ministry. But we come to understand through more
of Jesus' ministry and through more of Scripture that while baptism
includes the clear imagery of cleansing, it encompasses much more
theologically. And so we look even more deeply into the Scriptures.

We then find a passage at the end of the Gospel of Matthew where
Jesus' disciples gather around him on a mountain just before he
ascends into heaven. Jesus commissions them, "Go therefore and
make disciples of all nations, baptizing them in the name of the Father
and of the Son and of the Holy Spirit, and teaching them to obey
everything that I have commanded you" (Matthew 28:19-20). We
have interpreted this not only as a commission for all disciples,
including us today, but also as Jesus' preferred order for enacting the
rite. In other words, baptism should come after one is made into a disciple. Baptism requires faith because it serves as a response to the faith
that God gives us. We are to make disciples and baptize them. This
is our biblical heritage as Baptist Christians.

So, we might wonder, where did so many traditions in the Christian church get the idea of baptizing infants? The early church for several decades, we are convinced, was baptizing new adult believers only. The only historical or biblical arguments against this hypothesis are Scripture passages that record the entire household of a believer being baptized along with that person (Cornelius [Acts 10:44-48; 11:12-16], Lydia [Acts 16:14-15], the Philippian jailer [Acts 16:27-34], Crispus [Acts 18:8], and Stephanas [1 Corinthians 1:16]). One then must argue that the other members of the household included infants and children who did not believe, and that these children were among those in the household baptized.

Nevertheless, this is one of the best biblical arguments for paedobaptism. Proponents maintain that the notion of circumcision from the Old Testament (a rite for infant boys) is replaced by baptism in the covenant community of the church. And as a result, some time before the Middle Ages, the Christian church began to stress baptism at the beginning of natural birth rather than spiritual rebirth, roughly coinciding with an era when Christianity began to mark the stages of the physical life instead of the spiritual one.

The problem with these arguments is that they do not reflect the intent of Scripture. When Paul makes the comparison of circumcision to baptism, it comes under the rubric of this now being an act of faith, that this is a circumcision of the heart. The New Testament is a paradigm shift, then, from the physical to the spiritual. We are all children of God when we believe in him. It is a spiritual thing. And, "to put it succinctly," says R. Wayne Stacy, "Baptists disbelieve in surrogate faith. The encounter with God required for salvation and regeneration is necessarily an individual encounter."[4]

Others have argued for infant baptism on the basis of their future faith. But as the great Anabaptist theologian Balthasar Hubmaier remarked five centuries ago, a claim for a "future faith is really a mocking casuistry, for under no circumstances was that the institution of Christ." He argued,

It is the same thing to baptize infants for a future faith as to hang up a barrel hoop at Easter in hope of future wine which is not to be casked until fall, and of which one does not know whether it will be ruined beforehand by hail, or frost, or other kinds of storms. . . . What if the child grows up to be a fool? What kind of initial sign would baptism then be?[5]

How can it be spiritual, then, if the one being baptized is not yet old enough to believe? Thomas Helwys, one of the very first Baptists, warned Christians,

> What shall it profit you to have your infants washed with water and a few words whereby the name of the Lord is blasphemed, and you perish for so profaning his ordinances? The infant is never the better, it shall not be saved thereby, and there is no such obedience required at your hands. [Instead] let the word of the Lord be your guide in these things, and not the word of man nor long custom.[6]

Even some Baptists, in their eagerness to add to their baptism statistics, have begun to forget this Baptist heritage, and so they inappropriately baptize younger and younger children. One egregious example is a church in Arkansas that boasts a children's wing developed by Disney designer Bruce Barry that features video games, a light show, music videos, and even a bubble machine as part of weekly children's activities. But the real kicker is that this church, to encourage baptisms for kids, made a children's baptistery in the shape of a fire truck. As a child goes under the water, sirens blare and confetti is shot out of a canon. At first blush, this sounds like a great deal of fun, but churches must be careful about unintended and insidious consequences because young children, unable to take seriously the waters of baptism, might become part of the congregation simply for the fun of it.

The sad result of a trend toward earlier baptisms among Baptists is that more and more children are being baptized with more razzle-dazzle but without having any understanding of baptism's real meaning; they are emotionally excited, but they fail to see the significance of what was to have already happened spiritually in their heart. The point is that, in a way, they should be a little afraid of those baptismal waves. In fact, we all should. Because by being baptized, we are saying that we are willing to die to our old habits, to our long-held sins, to our old, comfortable, complacent selves. We have come to recognize that a spiritual funeral is in order for us.

But if we fail to recognize the gravity of this rite, if we make baptism merely a recreational activity in which others are coaxed to join in without comprehending the stakes involved, then we have actually watered-down water baptism! This kind of ecclesial behavior becomes so commonplace and acceptable that theological substance is eroded by cultural accommodation. And this is akin to what the early church did. By the end of the third century, baptism became increasingly incorporated into society and institutionalized in the church. It became something done by ordained priests to all laity and all citizens in a community.

Sixteenth-century Protestant Reformers such as Luther, Zwingli, Bucer, and Calvin began the great baptismal renewal by arguing that water baptism per se is not salivific, but rather is something that should be done as a means of grace from God. The Anabaptists, who are the Baptists' theological forebears, took it a step further by restoring the biblical witness. They argued that the church is not a part of culture and thus should remain separate from it. Indeed, only truly believing adults should be candidates for baptism and church membership. And later, English Baptists and others who looked back at the Greek New Testament rediscovered that the word *baptizō* means "to dip, immerse." Translators of the King James Bible, we have learned, actually coined the English word *baptism* in order to obscure this original meaning and to be in keeping with their practice of sprinkling rather than be faced with the implications of a literal rendering of the Greek word.

Although the amount of water required to make a baptism a baptism has been debated, and although the earliest Baptists actually did not immerse, Baptists generally have agreed over the centuries that the manifestation of faith should precede the rite of baptism. That is, people need to really understand and believe before they are baptized. And immersion best represents, symbolically, what God has done and promises to do for those who do believe in him. Paul says that we have been "buried with [Christ] in baptism" and "raised with him through faith in the power of God, who raised him from the dead" (Colossians 2:12), and that we have been "buried with [Christ] by baptism into death, so that, just as Christ was raised from the dead by the glory of the Father, so we too might walk in newness of life" (Romans 6:4).

The profile of one being immersed symbolizes burial in and resurrection from the tomb. The baptistery indeed becomes a kind of tomb. And as much as our society avoids conversations about death, until we recognize that reality, we are not ready for baptism. In fact, Baptists believe that a death in very much in order in those baptismal waves. A dramatic example comes from sixteenth-century Poland. The Brethren congregation of Rakow dug a baptismal pit to resemble an open grave and placed it on their cemetery mound along with other unmarked graves. This might be a bit too eerie to our contemporary tastes, but it makes the theological point. We believe that baptism symbolizes a kind of death, a death to old ways, to our old, sinful self.

The movie *The Piano* is about a nineteenth-century single mother, Ada. Motivated by the promise of an arranged marriage, Ada moves with her young daughter from Scotland to the New Zealand outback. Ada is mute, unable to speak since childhood. She lives in an emotional prison of shame and anger. Ada's sole source of pleasure is her piano, which she brought with her from Scotland.

In New Zealand, she marries a farmer who turns out to be abusive. A mysterious man, George, arranges then to take her away from the abusive marriage, to escape along with her daughter and her cherished piano. They are to make their getaway by sea. And as they row from shore toward an awaiting ship, the weight of the piano begins to sink their small boat. In just that moment, Ada suddenly gains insight into her life. She realizes that her piano is a symbol of her shame and regret. Ada signals to push the piano out of the boat.

"What did she say?" George asks her daughter, Flora.

"She says, throw the piano overboard," Flora replies.

Convinced that the piano could still be saved, George counters, "It's quite safe. They are managing."

More determined, Flora speaks on her mute mother's behalf. "She says throw it overboard. She doesn't want it. She says it's spoiled."

Finally, George gives in to Ada's request. But as the piano splashes into the sea, a rope tied to the piano encircles Ada's boot. Ada too is pulled into the water and sinks with the piano. She kicks and frees her foot from the boot, and then she frantically swims to the surface. When her head breaks the water's surface, she gasps her first breath as a free woman, released from the bondage of shame.[7]

Yes, the best baptisteries are not those made to look like fire trucks, or even those featuring nature scenes painted on the walls or in stained glass above them. The best baptisteries are those that look like tombs. When you step down into the water, you are moved to think of death, the death of your old, sinful life as you have known it.

A little boy was asked in Sunday school to explain baptism. He responded, "It's when the preacher holds you under water, and you think about Jesus." From the mouths of babes!

Baptism first means that we are willing to die. We die to ourselves, which means that we die to our old sins and those things that made us faithless to God. And we allow ourselves to be plunged helplessly beneath the water. The apostle Paul says that "all of us who were baptized into Christ Jesus were baptized into his death" (Romans 6:3). We renounce who we used to be and take on Christ instead. Our old self is crucified with Christ; our life of sin is drowned and destroyed so that its power over us might be broken. Our lives of corruption and sin and selfishness and all that had immerged in us are now immersed from us. Baptism spiritually demarcates the death of the old person who we have been up to this point. And it often takes such a ceremony for us to understand the level to which we need to change.

People who try to quit smoking or drinking have a terrible time of it no matter what they do (the addiction being so great). But George Mason points out that here many find that a ceremony of sorts is quite helpful. Putting yourself through a rite such as opening a pack of cigarettes or a bottle of liquor and flushing the contents down the toilet might just be the funeral you need to break the habit. Watching an old pleasure that was doing more harm than good be flushed away for good can have a powerful effect. Of course, you can run out to the store and buy more, but the fact that you deliberately put to death the habit with such powerful symbolism has a way of giving relief and courage to change and be changed by it.[8]

This is the power of baptism. It is taking something that is external and physical to represent something internal and spiritual. God knew that we need the ordinances—those outward signs—for this reason. We sometimes just have to see an object lesson outside of us to comprehend that which we cannot see inside of us. But there are always those in the Christian tradition who want to do away with the exterior ceremonies. They argue that we traditional Christians get so tied up in the outward trappings of Christian practice that we miss the point that faith concerns itself with looking not outwardly but inwardly, to the matters of the heart. And many of the newfangled contemporary community churches and low-key coffeehouse churches springing up here and there often are doing away with baptism. Like the Quakers before them, they stress the interior life instead. Faith, they argue, is a mysterious act of the Holy Spirit; it is something that happens within the inner life of a person. Baptism, by contrast, is a superfluous outer or exterior ceremony. The Christian life of faith is exclusively an internal sentiment. However, could we not argue the same thing about love?

As a college football fan, I can remember great episodes at dozens of games. But one occurrence I remember fondly from my college days happened not on the playing field, but up in the air and in the stands. At one game, an airplane was seen flying overhead with a banner attached. This banner did not carry the typical "Eat at Joe's Diner after the game" kind of message. Instead it said, "Jenny, I love you. Will you marry me?" One by one, fans diverted their attention from the game to the banner and then began scanning the stadium in search of the couple. We all found them halfway down the student section. Cheers erupted as the masses celebrated in Jenny's affirmation and public acceptance.

This is akin to baptism. It is going public with one's affection and its accompanying commitment. Here in baptism we pledge to follow the One who has expressed his love for us already. We make our formerly private affections public, and we affirm the relationship for all the world to see. It is like the little boy who asked pastor Rick Warren of Saddleback Church in California, "When can I get advertised?" What he meant, of course, was "baptized," but the theological point is roughly the same. Baptism becomes the advertisement that you, indeed, are a Christian. And Christians have been doing this rite no matter what the cost.

Jim Denison tells the story of when he was in college, serving as a summer missionary in East Malaysia. While he was there, he attended a small church. At one of the church's worship services a teenage girl came forward to announce her decision to follow Christ and be baptized. During the service, Denison noted some worn-out luggage against the wall of the church building, and he asked the pastor about it. The pastor pointed to the girl who had just been baptized and told Denison, "Her father said that if she were baptized as a Christian, she could never go home again. So she brought her luggage."

That is what baptism really means for all of us in a certain way. We are identifying ourselves with Christ, no matter what the cost, and we declare ourselves as his, turning from our old lives. And for many, that death to the old, to the past, is indeed a marked and sacrificial separation.

But baptism is not a burial alone. It comes also with a resurrection. Baptism's second point is that we are raised to new life; we are lifted from those waters. Here the apostle Paul reminds us, "If we have died with Christ, we believe that we will also live with him" (Romans 6:8). So if we have left our old ways and died to our old sins, then we are to be buried like Jesus in our identification with him. But, also like Jesus, on Easter Sunday we are raised to new life in him. As with so many other paradoxical things about the Christian faith, what looks like bad news is almost always good news. And the good news is this: God is in the business of raising the dead. We are raised as like Christ to live new lives with our Lord when we place our love, our lives, and our faith in him.

In one of my favorite movies, *The Shawshank Redemption*, the main character, Andy Dufresne, who has been wrongly accused, convicted, and imprisoned for the murders of his wife and her lover, finally finds his chance at escape. In one of the most exciting scenes, Andy breaks into a sewage pipe inside the bowels of his high-security correctional facility during a thunderstorm and crawls through the muck with a new suit wrapped in plastic and tied to his leg. Upon emerging in the open air outside the prison facility, he lifts his arms in crucifix form and allows the pouring rain to clean him. Now he begins life as a new man, with a new suit and identity.[9]

Just so, we experience the symbolically cleansing waters of baptism in order to receive our new identities. But in doing so, we also identify ourselves with the one who had committed no crimes, no sins. It was he who took our sins upon himself, who was baptized by John to identify fully with us, and who allows us to be identified now with him in just the same manner.

Christians often even receive new baptismal garments, like Andy Dufresne's new suit, to correspond with this new identity. We are freed and are identified only as Christ's. And so, baptism is a way of making our faith public and renouncing the old self and taking on the new. In these waters we declare ourselves for Christ and make public our new life among the people of God. And we do this corporately for that reason, so that we all might commit ourselves, as the Great Commission states, to teaching each new disciple all that God has commanded, and also so that we all might be reminded of our own baptism and the promise of our resurrection to come. You receive the blessing of your true Father, the honor of being a brother or sister in Christ, and the privilege of living in the family of God.

I remember a conversation in class one day when I was a student in seminary. We were sharing stories about our baptism. A fellow student began to tell the story about why he actually went forward to be baptized. He had witnessed the baptisms of many others before him in his church, and the pastor always leaned over to whisper something into each candidate's ear before doing the immersion. My friend just had to find out what that pastor's secret nugget of truth was. And so, for those "Gnostic" motivations primarily, he went forward. On the day of baptism, the pastor, as expected, cupped his hand over my friend's ear as he eased his way into the warm water. That secret doctrine, those sage words of truth? "Bend your knees, boy, bend your knees," the pastor simply said.

Why do Baptists make such a big deal about baptism? It is no secret, really, at all. In fact, it is quite the opposite. For through our baptism we make our faith public, proclaiming to our church, our community, and the world that we have been and are being saved by Christ Jesus. This salvation comes as a gift to us, an accomplished fact through the actual death and resurrection of Christ. Baptism, then, is our first act of faith and of imitating him. And Baptists know well that although baptism does not save us, it is our spiritual response to the one who does save us. And so Baptists for four centuries have taken the plunge to proclaim our faith in the "good old way."

In *A Small Treatise of Baptisme, or Dipping*, Baptist leader Edward Barber made this case for believer's baptism: "We are commanded to stand in the way, and aske for the old pathes, which is the good way and walke therein. . . . The old and good way under the Gospell is the Institution of Jesus Christ. . . . But the dipping of beleevers is that good old way of Christ."[10]

And so Baptists can indeed sing that Appalachian gospel song:

> *As I went down in the river to pray*
> *Studying about that good old way*
> *And who shall wear the starry crown*
> *Good Lord, show me the way!*
>
> *O sinners, let's go down,*
> *Let's go down, come on down,*
> *O sinners, let's go down,*
> *Down in the river to pray.*[11]

Notes

1. H. Leon McBeth gives the first two examples in his chapter "Baptists Before 1845," in *Baptists: History, Distinctives, Relationships*, ed. E. Eugene Greer Jr. (Dallas: Baptist General Convention of Texas, 1996), 4; and the latter two in his book *The Baptist Heritage: Four Centuries of Baptist Witness* (Nashville: B&H Academic, 1987), 48.

2. McBeth, *The Baptist Heritage*, 79.

3. Cited in George H. Shriver and Bill J. Leonard, eds., *Encyclopedia of Religious Controversies in the United States* (Westport, CT: Greenwood Press, 1994), 42.

4. R. Wayne Stacy, "Baptism," in *A Baptist's Theology*, ed. R. Wayne Stacy (Macon, GA: Smyth & Helwys, 1999), 166.

5. Balthasar Hubmaier, "On the Christian Baptism of Believers," in *Balthasar Hubmaier: Theologian of Anabaptism*, trans. and ed. H. Wayne Pipkin and John H. Yoder (Scottdale, PA: Herald Press), 118–19.

6. Thomas Helwys, "The Mystery of Iniquity," cited in *Baptist Roots: A Reader in the Theology of a Christian People*, ed. Curtis W. Freeman, James Wm. McClendon Jr, and C. Rosalee Velloso da Silva (Valley Forge, PA: Judson Press, 1999), 87.

7. The original story is from *The Piano* (Miramax Films, 1993), written and directed by Jane Campion. The illustration for baptism was developed by Greg Asimakoupoulos and Doug Scott in *Movie-Based Illustrations for Preaching and Teaching: 101 Clips to Show or Tell*, ed. Craig Brian Larson and Andrew Zahn (Grand Rapids: Zondervan, 1993), chapter 7.

8. My thanks to George A. Mason for this illustration. See Mason, "The Baptistry: Tomb and Womb," *The Wilshire Pulpit* (May 19, 1996), np.

9. *The Shawshank Redemption* (Castle Rock Entertainment, 1994). The original novella is by Stephen King, "Rita Hayworth and the Shawshank Redemption."

10. Cited in H. Leon McBeth, *A Sourcebook for Baptist Heritage* (Nashville: B&H Academic, 1990), 43.

11. "Down in the River to Pray," a traditional Appalachian gospel song, probably was written in the nineteenth century by G. H. Allan of Nashville and was first published in the hymnal *Southern Harmony*.

CHAPTER 12

A SERMON ON THE BAPTIST DISTINCTIVE OF
The Lord's Supper

The Church Body Remembering and Proclaiming the New Covenant

TODD D. STILL
1 Corinthians 11:17-34

I remember with some degree of clarity my earliest experiences with the Lord's Supper. I must have been about six years old. Seated on the padded pews of the First Baptist Church of Wichita Falls, Texas, next to my mother and my older brother, my mother would whisper to me, "When the Communion plates are passed to you, pass them along without taking anything." You see, I had not yet made a public profession of faith and been baptized. As a young child, I was particularly intrigued by those bits of bread and thimbles of juice that I was not supposed to eat or drink. Forbidden fruit, I thought.

After I confessed faith in Christ at the age of eight and was baptized into Christ and into the church at the age of nine, I began to ingest those awful-tasting wafers and to drink the sip of Welch's grape juice that followed. I recall thinking to myself that if you were meant to eat that bread, then you needed a lot more juice to wash away its taste. (I still think that.) Over time, my curiosity in Communion waned. The Baptist churches in which I worshiped and served did not seem to value the Lord's Supper all that much. It was observed infrequently and explained inadequately, at least in my memory.

Then came seminary and church history: transubstantiation, consubstantiation, symbolic memorial, real presence, sacrament, ordinance, elements. Open or closed communion? Weekly, monthly, or quarterly observance? The fascination returned. My interest was piqued all the more when I was denied the Eucharist in a Catholic Church and when I was served wine instead of Welch's at an Episcopalian Communion service.[1]

As a layperson and staff member of Baptist churches, I was afforded the luxury of thinking theoretically, or not at all, about the Lord's Supper. When I received the call to be the pastor of Uddingston Baptist Church in Uddingston, Scotland, in January 1993, however, I was forced to think through and not merely about this issue. That assembly of Christians observed Communion at the conclusion of worship every Sunday morning. Although some visitors excused themselves, the majority of the fellowship remained to receive the Lord's Supper. Deacons distributed chunks of hearty, tasty wheat bread before passing around an awful concoction made by Iris Marren—"Gran," as we called her. I reckon that Gran's potion was diluted juice or wine, but I never asked. I am not so sure that I wanted to know precisely what it was we were drinking, and I was not about to suggest that we change the traditional concoction.

So, to save myself, and perhaps some within the congregation, from the prison of the perfunctory, I set out to learn more about the Lord's Supper. To begin, I turned to Scripture. Before turning to councils and confessions, I remembered and recited to myself a basic Baptist battle cry: "No creed but the Bible." As a beginning pastor and a neophyte doctoral student in New Testament studies, I had far more questions than answers (I still do), but I did recall that the earliest and fullest account of the Lord's Supper is found in 1 Corinthians 11:17-34. It was to that text I first turned; it is where we now turn.

Having called the Corinthian women to pray and prophesy with their heads covered (another text for another time!), Paul proceeds to address congregational factions and divisions that were rearing their ugly heads at the Lord's Supper. In fact, Paul regarded the conflict to be so grave and the conduct so egregious that he maintains, "When you gather together, it is not the Lord's supper [*kyriakon deipnon*] that you eat" (11:20).[2]

It appears that some Corinthians were being overserved at the supper, while others were being underserved or, worse yet, not served at all. Perhaps a few of the wealthier members of the fellowship were gathering in a villa's triclinium, eating sumptuous foods and drinking desirable wines, while other Corinthians were left outside in the atrium to eat scraps and drink dregs, if they were lucky. If some were eating filet mignon and drinking port, others were choking down soybean burgers with the aid of watered-down wine.[3] However one reconstructs the sociohistorical situation into which Paul speaks, of this we may be certain: Paul was appalled. The text clearly shows his distress: "What! Do you not have houses in which to eat and drink? Or, do you despise the church of God and humiliate those who have nothing? What will I say to you? Will I praise you? In this I will not praise you!" (11:22).

Given the situation, Paul thinks it important, indeed imperative, to remind them of the so-called words of institution that he had previously delivered to them. After an introductory phrase in 11:23, Paul offers a summation of his earlier instruction to the Corinthians regarding the supper. He reminds them that it was on the night that Jesus was handed over or delivered up that he took, blessed, and broke bread and then said, "This is my body which is for you; this do [i.e., take, break, and bless bread] in my memory" (11:23b-24). After they ate, Paul continues recounting, Jesus took the cup and declared, "This cup is the new covenant in my blood. This do, as often as you may drink it [i.e., the contents of the cup], in my memory" (11:25). Even as Paul introduces his recitation of the words of institution with a brief remark, he concludes his account with this declaration: "For as often as you may eat this bread and drink the cup, the death of the Lord you proclaim until he might come" (11:26).

This passage requires thick commentary. Here, however, a few textual and theological remarks must suffice. To begin, one is struck by the christological texture of this passage. "Lord" appears in 11:23 and 11:26, and "Lord Jesus" occurs in 11:23. Furthermore, the pronouns "he" and "me/my" with reference to Christ are found four times respectively. Thus, there are no less than eleven references to Jesus in only four verses. Instructively, "I" and "you" bracket the passage but do not permeate it. If Jesus features in the text, his death in particular is front and center, as the Greek syntax of 11:26 indicates. Paul writes, *"ton thanaton tou kyriou katangellete."* The Lord's body is broken as bread; his blood is shed as wine is poured. "See from his head, his hands, his feet, / Sorrow and love flow mingled down; Did e'er such love and sorrow meet, / Or thorns compose so rich a crown?"[4]

In addition, 11:26 indicates that Paul regarded the eating of bread and the drinking of cup in the Lord's Supper to be a corporate proclamation of Jesus' crucifixion. It is the cross of Christ that Paul proclaimed when in Corinth. Paul puts it this way earlier in the letter: "For I determined to know nothing in your midst except Jesus Christ and him crucified" (2:2). Paul interprets the Lord's Supper elements as an ongoing preachment of the new covenant inaugurated through Jesus' grisly death on a Roman gallows. The bread and the cup are meant to remind us of the idiocy of preaching a crucified Christ, a source of shame to some and of scorn to others.[5] In Pauline parlance, seen at the beginning of this letter, Christ crucified is "a stumbling block to Jews and folly to Greeks, but to those who are called, both Jews and Greeks, Christ is the power of God and the wisdom of God" (1:23-24). In the Lord's Supper one is to encounter and exclaim power in weakness and wisdom in foolishness.

If the Lord's Supper is christological in content, it is ecclesial in context. The Lord's Supper is to be shared when the church, locally and concretely construed, assembles or comes together (note 11:18,20,33-34). Problems had arisen in the Corinthians' observation of the supper, and the splintering of the saints at the supper elicits a strong reaction from Paul. Some Corinthians were eating the bread and drinking the cup unworthily and were displaying a cavalier and callous disregard for their fellow believers. They were sullying the Lord's Supper by dishonoring other members of the body of Christ.

In the chapter to follow, Paul will write, "God has so composed the body . . . that there may be no discord in the body, but that the members may have the same care for one another. If one member suffers, all suffer together; if one member is honored, all rejoice together" (12:24-26). In 11:30-32 Paul goes so far as to say that many Corinthians are sick and a few have even died as a result of their reckless, heartless disinterest in other members of the body and the spiritual health of the assembly.[6] To be sure, this complex passage is perplexing, but this much is clear: the Lord takes seriously the sanctity of the supper.

Even as eschatological convictions inform Paul's statements about judgment relative to the Lord's Supper, they are also operative in his interpretation of it. He understands the community's eating of bread and drinking of cup to be a proclamation of the Lord's crucifixion until the Lord's coming, or parousia, a topic that Paul touches upon at the outset of 1 Corinthians and returns to in greater detail in chapter 15. If Paul can speak of the Lord's Table in terms of communion in 10:16, he does not do so in 11:26. Here, in fact, Paul does not link the supper with the Lord's presence; rather, he speaks of the supper in terms of the Lord's absence. It is something that the church practices and of which it partakes in the time between times. It is not until "the perfect comes" that "the partial will pass away" (13:10).

It is sometimes suggested that Baptists are Paulinists. This certainly seems to be the case with respect to the Lord's Supper. As Roger Olson points out in his helpful 2008 essay on the subject, unlike Christians in the Reformed, Lutheran, and Catholic traditions, Baptists have not typically thought of the Lord's Supper as an "outward eating" of Christ, either spiritually or bodily. Nor have Baptists, Olson suggests, usually considered it to be a sacrament in the sense that it offers a special means of grace.[7] That being said, one contemporary sacramentalist Baptist theologian, whom Olson quotes, contends that more "theological reflection is needed to facilitate a move from a theology of real absence to a theology of real presence [relative to the Lord's Supper]."[8] In response to this theologian's clarion call to view the Lord's Supper as a sacrament in a more technical sense, it is tempting to suggest that more careful exegetical consideration of 1 Corinthians 11:26 is needed before arriving at this conclusion.

To be fair and to be sure, any biblical theology of the Lord's Supper requires a treatment of all pertinent passages, including, but not limited to, John 6, where one encounters talk of eating Jesus' flesh and drinking Jesus' blood.[9] Be that as it may, Paul's interpretation of the supper should not be given short shrift. In fact, a strong argument can be made that as the earliest account of the Lord's Supper, it ought to be given pride of place. To those Corinthians who were claiming spiritual fullness, richness, and completeness, Paul cries, "Not yet!" He reminds them, "No eye has seen, nor ear heard, nor heart conceived, what God has prepared for those who love him" (2:9). Furthermore, he adds, "For now we peer into a mirror enigmatically, but then face to face; now I know in part, but then I will know fully even as I have been fully known" (13:12). Paul calls the Corinthians, and us, to join him in praying *Marana tha*, "Our Lord, come" (16:22). But until he comes, we are to keep breaking the bread, drinking the cup, and proclaiming the scandal that is the gospel.

I cherish those moments when exegesis and experience meet. One such moment occurred for me when I was a member of the First Baptist Church of Arlington, Texas, over ten years ago. In so many ways it was what I have come to know as a typical Lord's Supper service: pastor officiating, deacons distributing, musicians playing, people praying. Before the deacons dispersed to serve those curious little cubes of bread, however, I vividly recall the pastor, Dr. Charles Wade, telling them to "serve the people." At that moment, I gather, the Lord's Supper started to make more sense to me. The Lord's Supper, I thought, was and is about service. It is about a Lord who took up towel and basin (John 13:1-20). It is about a Lord who said, "The Son of Man did not come to be served but to serve and to give his life as a ransom for many" (Mark 10:45). It is about the Lord's people being reminded afresh of what their Lord was like so that they might be more fully like him.

Indeed, Communion is a proclamation, whereby the elements echo the cry of the Christ who said, "If anyone will come after me, let this one deny self, take up the cross daily, and follow me" (Luke 9:23). Communion leads to Calvary; communion leads to commitment. "Were the whole realm of nature mine, / That were a present far too small; Love so amazing, so divine, / Demands my soul, my life, my all."[10]

So, as we go about the daily living of our lives, let us become the sacraments that the Lord can break and bless to bring hope and healing to a hurting world until he comes. And when he comes, faith will be sight, foretaste will give way to glory, and supper will be served. I am told that it is going to be some shindig indeed, with all that you care to eat and to drink (see, e.g., Matthew 5:6; Revelation 7:16; cf. Isaiah 49:10). No one will be served scraps, and no one will have to drink dregs. Now *that* is the Lord's Supper!

Notes

1. For past and present Baptist perceptions and practices of the Lord's Supper, see Bill J. Leonard, *Baptist Ways: A History* (Valley Forge, PA: Judson Press, 2003), and Roger E. Olson, "The Baptist View," in *The Lord's Supper: Five Views* (Downers Grove, IL: InterVarsity Press, 2008), 91–108.
2. Translations of New Testament texts are my own.
3. For scholarly support for such a scenario, see Gerd Theissen, *The Social Setting of Pauline Christianity: Essays on Corinth*, ed. and trans. John H. Schütz (Edinburgh: T & T Clark, 1982), 145–74.
4. This is the third stanza of Isaac Watts's beloved hymn, "When I Survey the Wondrous Cross."
5. See further Martin Hengel, *Crucifixion in the Ancient World and the Folly of the Message of the Cross*, trans. John Bowden (Philadelphia: Fortress, 1977).
6. For an insightful, succinct treatment of 1 Corinthians 11:27-34, see Richard B. Hays, *First Corinthians*, Interpretation Bible Commentary (Louisville: John Knox, 1997), 201–3.
7. See Olson, "The Baptist View."
8. Ibid., 107.
9. See Ben Witherington III, *Making a Meal of It: Rethinking the Theology of the Lord's Supper* (Waco, TX: Baylor University Press, 2007).
10. This is the fourth stanza of Isaac Watts's hymn, "When I Survey the Wondrous Cross."

A Free Church in a Free Land

Religious Liberty and the Separation of Church and State

Religious Liberty

Perhaps the most distinctive mark of the believers' church movement, next only to credobaptism, is its plea for religious liberty, not just for churches and Christians with similar beliefs, but for all citizens of the nations in which it has abided. The call for religious toleration came as early as 1524 when Anabaptist theologian Balthasar Hubmaier argued on behalf of the persecuted minorities in Europe that "the inquisitors are the greatest heretics of all, because counter to the teaching and example of Jesus they condemn heretics to fire; and before it is time they pull up the wheat together with the tares. ... Therefore to burn heretics appears to be confessing Christ (Titus 1:16), but indeed it is to deny him."[1] However, Anabaptists and Baptists did not stop at insisting on mere toleration. As the great twentieth-century Baptist preacher George W. Truett stirringly proclaimed from the steps of the United States capitol building:

> Baptists have one consistent record concerning liberty throughout all their long and eventful history. They have never been party to oppression of conscience. They have forever been the unwavering champions of liberty, both religious and civil. Their contention now is, and has been, and, please God, must ever be, that it is the natural and fundamental and indefeasible right of every human being to worship God or not, according to the dictates of his conscience, and, as long as he does not infringe upon the rights of others, he is to be held accountable alone to God for all religious beliefs and practices. Our contention is not for mere toleration, but for absolute liberty. ... It is the consistent and insistent contention of our Baptist people, always and everywhere, that religion must be forever voluntary and uncoerced, and that it is not the prerogative of any power, whether civil or ecclesiastical, to compel men to conform to any religious creed or form of worship, or to pay taxes for the support of a religious organisation to which they do not belong and in whose creed they do not believe. God wants free worshippers and no other kind.[2]

Religious liberty, then, is seen by Baptists to be an extension of their tenet of the freedom of conscience. And in the sermon on the topic of religious liberty to follow, Ronald Cook highlights the founding of George W. Truett Theological Seminary, an institution named for one of the greatest Baptist proponents of religious liberty in the modern period.

The Separation of Church and State

To protect against the infringement of such liberty, Baptists have also insisted on the principle of the separation of church and state. As early as 1611 Baptists declared, "The magistrate, by virtue of his office, is not to intermeddle with religion, or matters of conscience, nor to compel men to this or to that form of religion or doctrine; but to leave the Christian religion to the free conscience of every one, and to meddle only with political matters. . . . Christ alone is the King and lawgiver of the Church and conscience."[3] Thus, though technically they are different doctrines, religious liberty is inextricably tied to the Baptist principle of the separation of church and state. Although Baptists have disagreed not only with other religious traditions but also among themselves about the meaning of this separation, most Baptists affirm some sense of the idea that civil government is restricted in its sovereignty to legal and secular matters, leaving matters of faith and conscience to the church and each individual citizen. All these matters are predicated on the notion that each person is free to believe in God according to personal volition, and correspondingly, each individual will one day be answerable to God for personal choices, beliefs, and behavior. If each person is answerable, then each person must not be compelled by any outer force to worship, to believe, and to live the faith except according to the dictates of his or her own conscience.

Baptists have intrepidly stood for these principles since their inception as a persecuted minority in England. In 1614 Leonard Busher presented to the king and Parliament a treatise entitled "Religious Peace, or a Plea for Liberty of Conscience," which may well have been the first proposal for religious liberty in the English language.[4]

Through their subsequent confessions, treatises, and political appeals, Baptists sought and ultimately found greater acceptance of religious liberty not only for themselves, but also for every religious group both in England and in the American colonies.

Baptists in America, including Roger Williams, Isaac Backus, and John Leland, argued against state-supported religion, fighting not only for the release of unlicensed clergy from prison, but also against colonial taxation on all citizens for support of one brand of religion. Backus wrote, "Nothing is more evident, both in reason and the Holy Scriptures, than that religion is ever a matter between God and individuals, and, therefore, no man or men can impose any religious test without invading the essential prerogatives of our Lord Jesus Christ."[5] One can easily see that the Baptist apprehension of the individual understanding of faith, the soul competency of each believer, the freedom of conscience, and religious liberty are inextricably tied to one another in Baptist thought.

Thomas Jefferson ultimately supported the Baptist appeal, convincing his own Virginia General Assembly to accept his Bill for Religious Freedom in 1785. Baptists were greatly aided in this pioneering effort by other dissenting religious groups such as Presbyterians, Catholics, and Quakers. Baptists subsequently encouraged and supported Jefferson and James Madison to take the same measures of religious protection to the federal level to advocate for complete religious liberty for all Americans. That the first amendment to the U.S. Constitution provided no religious test clause and prohibited the government from intervening in religious matters, Robert Torbet notes, "was due in no small part to the agitation of New England and Virginia Baptists."[6]

It is worth noting that upon his inauguration as the third president of the United States, Thomas Jefferson received a letter in 1801 from the Danbury Baptist Association (Connecticut) expressing concern that complete religious liberty was yet to be established in all the state constitutions, including their own. They eloquently appealed the new president, saying, "Our hopes are strong that the sentiment of our beloved President, which have had such genial effect already, like the radiant beams of sun, will shine and prevail through all these States."[7] Jefferson famously responded,

> Believing with you that religion is a matter which lies solely between man and his God, that he owes account to none other for his faith or his worship, . . . I contemplate with sovereign reverence that act of the whole American people which declared that their legislature

would 'make no law respecting an establishment of religion, or prohibiting the free exercise thereof,' thus building a wall of separation between church and state.[8]

To be clear, historians and constitutional experts debate whether the Bill of Rights actually established a "wall of separation" and, if so, the nature of what that wall was intended to protect. Nevertheless, Jefferson's words came as assurance to Baptists that at the very least the state would no longer meddle in religious matters. Thus, Baptists and other religious groups have enjoyed the separation of church and state in the United States for over two centuries. In like manner, Baptists throughout the world have urged governments to foster religious freedom and protect dissenting religious groups and the individual freedom of conscience.

Baptists have fervently believed that, given freedom for every religious group, the Baptist witness will prosper by the work of the Holy Spirit. But as Alan Lefever describes in his sermon on the separation of church and state to follow, as Baptists have become a dominant religious tradition in the last century, the temptation to succumb to the power of hegemony must not overcome the Baptist principles for soul competency and religious freedom for the use of government force to compel faith and its practice. As Baptists have become a majority in some pockets of American culture, the lure to return to established religion must be defeated by the Baptists' own measured words: "God wants free worshippers and no other kind."

Notes

1. Balthasar Hubmaier, "On Heretics and Those Who Burn Them," nos. 13, 28, cited in H. Wayne Pipkin and John H. Yoder, *Balthasar Hubmaier: Theologian of Anabaptism* (Scottdale: Herald Press, 1989), 62, 64.

2. George W. Truett, "Baptists and Religious Liberty," in *God's Call to America: And Other Addresses Comprising Special Orations Delivered on Widely Varying Occasions* (New York: George H. Doran, 1923), 32–33.

3. John Smyth, "On Religious Liberty," cited in *Baptist Confessions of Faith*, William L. Lumpkin, ed. (Philadelphia: Judson Press, 1959), 140.

4. See George C. Lorimer, *The Baptists in History* (Boston: Silver, Burdett, 1893), 85–86.

5. Cited in Forrest Church, ed., *The Separation of Church and State: Writings on a Fundamental Freedom by America's Founders* (Boston: Beacon Press, 2004), 19.
6. Robert G. Torbet, *A History of the Baptists* (Valley Forge, PA: Judson Press, 1963), 243.
7. Church, *Separation of Church and State*, 128–29.
8. Thomas Jefferson, "Letter to the Danbury Baptist Association," cited in ibid., 130.

Action Steps for the Reader

1. For further reading on religious liberty and the state:

Church, Forrest, ed. *The Separation of Church and State: Writings on a Fundamental Freedom by America's Founders.* Boston: Beacon Press, 2004.

Estep, William R. *Revolution within the Revolution: The First Amendment in Historical Context, 1612–1789.* Grand Rapids: Eerdmans, 1990.

Kidd, Thomas S. *God of Liberty: A Religious History of the American Revolution.* New York: Basic Books, 2010.

Pfeffer, Leo. *Church, State, and Freedom.* Boston: Beacon Press, 1953.

2. Biblical texts for preaching and topical Bible study:

Matthew 17:24-27; 22:15-21; John 8:32; Acts 4:19-20; 22:25-29; Romans 6:6-18; 13:1-7; Galatians 5:1; 1 Timothy 2:1-6; 1 Peter 2:12-17; 2 Peter 2:19-22.

3. Idea for worship:

Make the Sunday that falls closest to Independence Day a day to preach on religious liberty and the spiritual liberty that Christians have through Christ. Recount the stories of the Baptist contribution to religious liberty by reading an account in worship or during the sermon.

4. Opportunity for service:

Form a partnership with other faith communities and organizations in your community and organize a "liberty walk" on an appropriate day in your community (e.g., election day, Independence Day) with the purpose of celebrating religious freedom and liberty of conscience.

CHAPTER 13

Religious Liberty

A New Legacy of Religious Liberty

RONALD L. COOK
Isaiah 56:3-7; Galatians 5:1-15

The dream of a new Baptist seminary was born in the minds and hearts of freedom-loving Texas Baptists in 1990, and steps were immediately taken to make this dream a reality. Baylor University president Dr. Herbert H. Reynolds reserved the name "George W. Truett Theological Seminary" on July 24, 1990, in the first of several intriguing moves to secure freedom for scholars and students on the campus of Baylor University in Waco, Texas. The dream became a reality when Truett Seminary opened with a founding faculty and her first class of students during the fall term, 1994.

It can be argued that the rather remarkable story of this new seminary could not have unfolded anywhere else at that particular time in history. What has become a new and vibrant center for Baptist theological education, with significant growth in faculty, students, and staff, was spawned in a tributary of religious liberty that was still flowing at full force among moderate Texas Baptists at that time. This stream had seen a constant flow among freedom-loving Baptists since their arrival in Texas in or before 1820. This stream, which seems at times to have slowed to a trickle, even among Texas Baptists, was still flowing strong as Truett was about to open its doors.

Texas Baptists, particularly those with an ethos centered and affiliated with Baylor University, had avoided in large measure the ideologically driven takeover of the Southern Baptist Convention (SBC) during the 1980s and early 1990s, at least with regard to Texas Baptist colleges (the SBC-owned Southwestern Baptist Theological Seminary had fallen in the early 1990s to the takeover movement). Texas Baptists were already talking about the need for a free seminary when events on the national level at SBC annual meetings intensified efforts of various kinds. Dr. Reynolds had established himself as a visionary and trusted leader for Baylor and a major statesman among Baptists in Texas and across the South. He had led Baylor to gain its freedom from denominational control with a series of deft and decisive moves in 1990–1991. It seems now that all he had to do was engineer the launching of this new theological vessel, and a new seminary was underway. On the basis of the inspiration and the stream of liberty within which this new seminary came to life, you might say that Truett Seminary was born of the water and the Spirit and with unreserved support of freedom-loving Baptists in Texas.

The details of the story are still told as full of fascinating intrigue and adept strategies. In a recent *Christianity Today* interview, Rob Bell, calling for a Christian alternative to violence and force, said that the "way of Jesus is always asking if there is an imaginative, subversive, brilliant, creative path."[1] We have the privilege of saying that Truett Seminary at its inception was removed from the denominational conflict that was still raging at that time, and so far this has been true. The reason is that a visionary and bold leader, Dr. Herbert Reynolds, took a better way that was indeed imaginative, subversive, brilliant, and creative.

What Is the Source of This Deep Spring of Religious Liberty?

Baptists have often based the ethos of freedom in the free and life-giving nature of God and in a vital relationship with God, emerging fully in the liberating salvation found in Jesus Christ. Substantially formed concepts of religious liberty can be found as early as the post-exilic thinking in Isaiah 56. The words have much in common with free Baptistic souls, announcing essentially the freedom to anyone who will come to live faithfully before Yahweh. Do not restrain the eunuch (56:4) who could not keep the laws of circumcision. Do not prohibit foreigners (56:3) with no Israelite genealogy to claim. To them, God says, his people must send the message, "Come unto me." The Lord declares, "My house shall be called a house of prayer for all peoples" (56:7).

Yahweh's directives are forceful: remove all barriers—personal, national, racial, cultic, religious—and let everyone freely come. And in those words so important to Jesus, found a bit down the scroll in Isaiah 61:1-2, the Lord says, "Let them freely go." God declares that all walls must come down, and that we must be advocates and liberators that all may have full liberty to come to the Lord and to go, living out life freely under the Lord.

Eventually followers of Christ would find that only in the cross of Christ did all barriers finally fall, and through Jesus Christ all can come for salvation and full liberation and receive the gift of life that he provides. All may come, unconstrained and unrestrained. All may go in newfound liberty and live out this life of faith without any constraint of any control by state, ecclesiastical body, or enforced creed.

So God's people are people of full spiritual and religious freedom, are we not? Well, from the earliest days until now it has not worked out that way. In New Testament accounts in Acts and in the letters of the apostle Paul we clearly see the other reality, and, with apologies to the comic strip character Pogo, "We have met the enemy, and he is us."

Brothers and sisters in Christ seemingly struggle to allow for full freedom in Christ. The situation among the Galatian churches shows that early on there were those who would shackle freedom. The situation among those churches was that some who had found life in Christ felt under obligation to enforce Jewish interpretation and application of Torah instruction. This led to a digression from the freedom made possible in Christ (Galatians 5:1) to the sad reality of biting and devouring, and contention born of the battle for conformity, which could lead to mutual destruction (Galatians 5:15).

So our freedom is born in the desire of God that all may come, and fully born to all who come to Christ. And yet, across the centuries it is a freedom for which freedom-loving followers of Christ have had to fight and, I believe, have had to do so in imaginative, subversive, brilliant, and creative ways.

What Does Religious Liberty Look Like?

We have already noted that religious liberty looks like the current version of the Baptist story being told by Truett Seminary. But it is an older story.

We must acknowledge that it looks like Balthasar Hubmaier and his wife and other Anabaptists who were martyred for radically living out their faith. In them it took an antimajoritarian form. Hubmaier contended, as would true Baptists across the centuries, for all minorities, both believers and unbelievers—even heretics and Turks, as he called them. One would hope that even those Baptists who will not claim the direct legacy of these Baptistic followers of Christ could acknowledge the influence of the stream of religious liberty that bubbles up among the Anabaptists.

It looks like John Smyth and Thomas Helwys seeking to establish a band of free Baptistic souls in the Netherlands, and then England. It looks like Roger Williams being banished from the Massachusetts Bay Colony to found a "lively experiment" as called for in his charter of radical and unrestrained religious liberty in the new colony of Rhode Island. It looks like John Leland of Virginia, friend of James Madison. It was Leland and other Baptists in Virginia who forged common ground with Madison and Thomas Jefferson and brokered votes in Virginia for the new U.S. Constitution only when Madison agreed to see a high view of religious liberty contained within the Bill of Rights to the Constitution.

In early Texas it looked like Noah T. Byars, in whose blacksmith shop in Independence, Texas, the Declaration of Independence of the Republic was signed. What is the significance of such a plain old Baptist? After battling as an armorer for Sam Houston's forces, he answered a call to preach the gospel and form churches in the frontier villages of Texas—Corsicana, Waco, and Brownwood. This champion of civic and religious liberty in early Texas Baptist life joined quite a cohort of missionaries to establish congregations of free Baptists in communities throughout the settled areas of early Texas. It is no coincidence that from these churches emerged the greatest champions of religious liberty among Baptists of the twentieth century: E. Y. Mullins from Corsicana; George W. Truett, who adopted Waco and then Dallas; and J. M. Dawson, who left the pastorate of the First Baptist Church in Waco to lead the Baptist Joint Committee on Public Affairs into prominence in the nation's capital after World War II and into the 1950s—the entity that Representative Chet Edwards calls the most significant advocate for religious liberty on the horizon.

I will mention one moment in the great career of E. Y. Mullins, known to most for his leadership at the Southern Baptist Theological Seminary in Louisville. His views have become quite controversial among some Baptists in recent years. This account came to me personally from Louie D. Newton of Georgia. One fall day in 1982 I sat in Newton's rocking chair in Atlanta. Those who know the history of Baptists in the South will recognize Newton as the patriarch of Georgia Baptists through the middle decades into the twentieth century and the man chosen to preach at the funeral of George W. Truett.

In one of many conversations, Louie Newton told me of an opportunity that came to him during his first months as the youngest editor of a state Baptist paper. E. Y. Mullins wired Newton, who was still in his early twenties, a brilliant young journalist recently chosen to be editor of Georgia Baptists' *Christian Index*, to ask that he bring his portable typewriter and accompany him on a trip to Stockholm. They would travel in July 1923, and Newton would accompany Mullins on the trip and be his personal secretary. This would make it possible for Mullins to prepare one of the most magnificent addresses on religious liberty ever delivered before the Baptist World Alliance.

They checked into a hotel room in Stockholm for a five-day stay, with Mullins scheduled to give his address on the last day. As Newton told the story, Mullins returned to his room every night, stripped to his comfortable underclothing for those hot nights, and began to pace the room. Newton said that every word poured forth from a deep well of a heart set free. On the first night, he dictated the speech to Newton and asked him to read it back. Newton said that it seemed perfect, and on the first reading it made his heart burn for freedom. Mullins took that manuscript, looked at it, and tore it up. He repeated this same routine every night, dictating almost verbatim the same speech from the night before, yet changing the nuance and strengthening the force at every strategic point. And every night before the last, he took the manuscript, which Newton had faithfully typed, and tore it up. On the last night, Newton said that the words poured forth from Mullins with incredible passion. Mullins spoke slowly, and Newton got every word with exacting correctness. When Mullins read the final copy, he pronounced, "This is it, Newton." And Mullins entered the hall the next night to address Baptists from all over the world, some from countries liberated just a few years earlier during World War I. It was a great moment for free Baptists.

Newton reported that Mullins's address on religious liberty lit fires in the hearts of all who were present and brought the crowd to its feet with its closing words:

> Human history has seen the downfall of many false authorities in Church and State. Crowns have been shattered and thrones sometimes broken down. But men have gathered the pieces of the broken thrones and they are erecting another greater than all, and they are making of the shattered crowns another more glorious than all. On that throne they are placing Jesus Christ, and that glorious crown they are putting on his brow, and I can hear by the ear of faith the far away rising and falling of the mighty chorus of nations: —
> "All hail the power of Jesus' name,
> Let angels prostrate fall;
> Bring forth the royal diadem,
> And crown Him, Lord of all."

This refrain of one Baptist announcing the freedom of all to come by faith and to worship with an unbridled heart and a liberated voice must have sounded wonderful, especially to those newly liberated from tyrannical powers.

Religious liberty looks like E. Y. Mullins. It looks like Louie D. Newton, who, with George W. Truett, led toward the first large integrated gathering in the South at the Baptist World Alliance meeting in Atlanta in 1939. We should treasure the legacy of freedom-seeking Baptists.

But what is at the heart of such a Baptist? I am convinced that it is an abiding confidence in one thing: a personal encounter with the liberating Christ that gives way to the privilege and power of the unshackled witness. It is the confidence that one who has found life and freedom in Christ needs to be unleashed. It is the confidence that an unleashed witness will convince many others. It is the confidence that an unshackled prophetic voice brings a corrective that no law, creed, or magisterium can ever deliver. It is the confidence that a preacher under only one constraint—the Spirit of our Lord—is the most powerful force for the gospel of Jesus Christ on this earth. It is not an ethos that will give in to a few forging the many into conformity. But it is the confidence that the soul set free in Christ will burst into a flame of Pentecostal proportions.

Does it carry the risk of some error? Of course. But just as the apostle Paul called for mutual service rather than destructive battles among the churches in Galatia, free Baptists have found that free and open men and women, with an open Bible and mutual accountability, will usually achieve common ground and inspire one another to great work. Thus Baptists, born in religious liberty, are a force, not a fort, for Jesus and his gospel.

What does it look like to be a free Baptist? I hope and pray that it looks like us. And that chapter is being written right now, so I guess we will see.

Note

1. "The Giant Story: Rob Bell on Why He Talks about the Good News the Way He Does," April 22, 2009 (http://www.christianitytoday.com/ct/2009/april/26.34.html).

CHAPTER 14

A SERMON ON THE BAPTIST DISTINCTIVE OF THE
Separation of Church and State

Baptists and the Myth of the "Myth"

ALAN J. LEFEVER
Matthew 22:15-22

The separation of church and state is a principle that distinguished Baptists from most other Christian groups when the movement began in 1609. Yet today there are those who call themselves Baptists who argue against this principle and say that this concept was never supported by Scripture, our Baptist founders, or this country's early leaders. To gauge society's perception of Baptists and the separation of church and state, I turned to the one source that has all of the answers, Wikipedia. And when I went to Wikipedia and typed in "Baptists and separation of church and state," I found, to my amazement, an article on the topic. It started with the line "Originally Baptists supported separation of church and state." I was stunned. "Originally"?

Meaning versus Exact Words

The word "originally," no doubt, had been put in this article because there are people who travel around today and speak in churches and associational meetings and gatherings and talk about the myth of separation, that our founders never meant for church and state to be separate, that what people have been told about separation of church and state is untrue. I thought, what is the difference between meaning and exact words? Because these people who build their case for the myth of separation of church and state point out that the phrase is not used in Scripture. I could not help but think back to when I was a boy, and one day my mother left for work and said to me, "Alan straighten up the house while I'm gone." I looked around the house and noticed nothing appeared to be crooked, so I reorganized the magazines and did a few other things. When she got home she looked around and said, "Why didn't you clean the living room? Why did you not clean the bathroom?" And I replied, "You didn't tell me to clean; you said straighten." Of course, I knew exactly what she had meant. I was just hoping that I could get by.

Jesus never used the phrase "separation of church and state," but certainly in Matthew 22:15-22 he addressed the matter. What a wonderful passage! The Pharisees think that they have it all figured out. They have the perfect plot. They are going to put Jesus in a situation where he has to answer yes or no. However, rather than ask the question themselves, they make sure that their disciples ask it, which gives the Pharisees a little bit of deniability. But first the disciples try to butter him up a little: "You are so brilliant, Jesus. You know so much. You answer everything, and what you say is what you think. It is the truth. So we want to ask you this question: Should we pay taxes to the Roman emperor?" And Jesus says, "Anybody got a coin?" (I can picture a parlor magician: "Anybody have a dollar? Anybody have a coin I can use?") And when they produce it, Jesus asks, "Whose image is on the coin?" "Caesar's," they answer. His response, "Give to Caesar what is Caesar's, and to God what is God's," was a stunner. Matthew reports that they were "amazed." Today we might say that they were dumbfounded. They had a "Bill and Ted moment," like in movie *Bill and Ted's Excellent Adventure*. They just sat there and thought, "Wow! There's no good comeback for that." Why? Because they had never heard anything like it. No one had ever talked about church and state being separate. No one had ever talked about there being two realms that we should live in where we have responsibilities and roles in both but the two are not united. They were expecting a simple yes or no, and all they got was further confused.

The apostles Peter and Paul, in other parts of the New Testament, certainly speak of the Christian's role in government, and how the civil government has authority in orderly living. But nowhere in the New Testament is there a call for the civil government to submit to religious leaders. And nowhere in the New Testament is there a call for religious leaders or believers to surrender their faith to the government. Nowhere. Instead, there certainly seems to be an implicit calling of separation of church from the state.

Our Baptist forebears certainly had something to say about the separation of church and state. In fact, if I wanted to, I could present page after page of quotations from Baptists dealing with separation of church and state. But let us begin in 1611, with one of the Baptist founders, Thomas Helwys, who wrote a work entitled *A Short Declaration of the Mystery of Iniquity*, which addresses religious liberty. Helwys was so confident that what he had to say was important that he autographed a copy of his work for the king, writing, "You, king, are a mortal man, not God, and have no power over immortal souls of your subjects." Of course, the king was so impressed to get this autographed copy that he wanted to locate Thomas Helwys so that he could thank him, which he did by throwing him into prison. If the king ever needed to talk to Helwys about religious liberty, he would know where to find him.

In 1640 Roger Williams, one of the first Baptists in America, said that there had been a hedge or a wall separating the paradise or the garden of the church from the wilderness of the state. This hedge or wall had been damaged and torn down over the years, and there was a need to rebuild and restore it so that the church could be restored to its rightful place and relationship to the state. This is an amazing thing: Roger Williams used the illustration of a wall in 1640. That is a little bit before the U.S. Constitution.

The people who peddle the theory that the separation of church and state is a myth like to point out that Thomas Jefferson, who gets credit for the phrase "separation of church and state," does not use the phrase when the Constitution is developed. He actually uses the phrase for the first time, as far as we can tell, in 1802. Whom is he addressing when he uses the phrase? How does it come about? He happens to be writing to a group of Baptists who are concerned about the government's relationship to the church. And in this letter, by noting that there is a wall of separation, he tries to calm the fears of these

Baptists who are worried that the government might infringe on their freedoms. The government should not have any impact on the church, and the people of the church will not be dictated to—how they live, how they carry out their tasks.

Several years later, James Madison, the author of the First Amendment, which contains the "establishment clause" protecting freedom of religion, took the same stance that Jefferson took. In 1811 he talked about there being a practical distinction between religion and civil government, essentially to purify both. He knew that there was a danger when church and state were not separate.

Admittedly, these words of the founders were not made in 1787 or in 1790, when the Constitution or the Bill of Rights were being developed and ratified. They came years later. But these are people who were intimately involved in the development of the Constitution and Bill of Rights. And, as we saw, there was Roger Williams, already speaking of a wall separating the church from the state in 1640.

And then there is a man with whom we should all be familiar, George W. Truett. Truett said in his memorable speech on the steps of the U.S. capitol building in 1920, "'Render unto Caesar the things that are Caesar's and unto God the things that are God's' is one of the most revolutionary and history making utterances that ever fell from the lips Divine. That utterance, once and for all, marked the divorcement of church and state. It marked a new era for creeds and deeds of men." Regardless of the words used, Baptist heritage is replete with examples of the necessity of the New Testament principle that we call "the separation of church and state." You can call it a myth if you like, but you cannot gloss over the fact that George W. Truett himself, a man revered by many people who view the separation of church and state as a myth, saw in Matthew 22:15-22 a decree of divorce between church and state.

Activism versus Isolationism

Some of these people who sell the myth of separation of church and state say that if Christians separate the church from the state, they isolate the church, and thus the church will have no impact on the world. But Baptist heritage tells another story. During his time in prison, Thomas Helwys had time to expound further upon his views expressed in *A Short Declaration of the Mystery of Iniquity* concerning the king's role as head of the government and the citizen's role in following the leadership of the king. However, Helwys made a clear distinction between the citizen, and in his case the Baptist citizen, when it came to religious matters. He believed that all citizens operated in two different realms: one under the leadership of the king, the other under the leadership of God. When Oliver Cromwell led the army in England in the 1640s and 1650s, Baptists became known as great fighters and patriots of the Parliamentary army. From that time until the present, Baptists have been known as good fighters, and not only on the battlefield.

Baptists in America were active in politics as well and helped to build the foundation of this country. Isaac Backus, who was appointed by the Warren Association's Grievance Committee to deal with legislative matters with the government, saw his own mother imprisoned for being a Baptist. When he went before the Massachusetts legislature while fighting for religious liberty in the separation of church and state, he noted that religious matters are to be separated from the jurisdiction of the state.

But although religious matters were separate, this did not mean that Baptists were removed from the political arena as they fought for religious liberty. In fact, to guarantee the importance of religious liberty, Isaac Backus went before the Massachusetts legislature in 1770, saying, in essence, "We need freedom; and if we do not get freedom, we are going to send an emissary to London and tell them what is going on, and they may want to do some research into it themselves." Legislators knew that if the English government "did some research," they would find that what was going on was the beginning stages of a revolution. Massachusetts backed off after realizing that irritating the Baptists was not a good idea. In 1774 Backus went back before the Massachusetts legislature and pointed out that Baptists were going to stop paying taxes to the Congregational Church of Massachusetts, which they neither attended nor supported. And the reason for the stoppage of paying taxes was that it was taxation without representation. Obviously, that way of stating it resonated with the Massachusetts legislature. The legislature did not act against the Baptists; they could not act against the Baptists because they would soon need them.

Many know the story of John Leland, the great Baptist from Virginia who, along with other Baptists, noted that there was no protection of religious liberty in the Constitution while it was being developed. Legend has it that he met with James Madison. Exactly how or where this meeting occurred we do not know. We do know that they communicated. We do not know if John Leland said, "If you do not get this straightened out, I am going to run against you for a seat in the Virginia Convention to ratify the Constitution." Or perhaps he said that someone else would run against Madison. We do know that John Leland made it clear to Madison that if he wanted to count on the swing vote of Baptists to get elected to the Constitutional Convention, he had to address their concerns about religious liberty. That is political activism. There is no removal or isolation when you are politically active. Saying that there is a separation of church and state does not mean that Christians should have nothing to do with what is going on in the world, that they should remove themselves from the political arena. In fact, Christians should always work to influence the world, to make it a better place.

In the early 1900s people around the United States who could see that the world was headed toward unprecedented conflict began holding peace conferences around the country to try to pull the world back from the brink of war. At the 1907 Texas Peace Conference, George W. Truett addressed the gathering and noted that in the last ten years the American population had increased by 10 percent, while military spending had increased by 300 percent. Truett asked his audience how much better the world could be if that money was used for the needy instead of the military. This happened not in 2010, but in 1907. And this was no left-wing radical, but George W. Truett. Why did Truett make this observation? Because he was saying that, as Christians, we must influence our society. We must make a difference. But there is a difference between having an influence in the world in which we live and having a union of church and state. Truett was so politically active in his career as pastor of First Baptist Church of Dallas that at least three times people approached him about running for the U.S. Senate. Why? Because he had influence, because people listened to what he said. So there is a record of Baptists throughout American history being active in politics, trying to help shape our society, yet still working for a separation of church and state.

The Boiling Pot

My wife and I love to go to Maine. We vacation there every October. The first question everybody asks us when we go to Maine is "Do you eat lobster?" Neither of us can stand it. It just never occurs to us to eat lobster, but in Maine you see lobsters everywhere. Of course, you hear the story about how lobsters are cooked. And some people will tell you that being boiled alive does not hurt the creatures at all, that in warm water they just get so relaxed, and the next thing you know, they are gone. I think sometimes there is the seduction of that warm water for Baptists today. On any Sunday morning you can go into many Baptist churches and find in the sanctuary a Christian flag on one side and an American flag on the other. I think that it is important for us to appreciate our country; I also think that it is one thing to worship God and appreciate our country and a completely different thing to worship God and worship our country. Today many Baptists have fallen into that temptation of the warm water of thinking "Yes, let us worship this country that God has ordained to be the greatest country in the world." God has not ordained us to be the greatest country in the world. He has asked and called us as Christians to make the world a better place. That is what we should strive for.

John Leland observed that the union of church and state never happens without the influence of the clergy. Today we have Baptists, or at least those who call themselves Baptists, working for things such as school prayer and school vouchers. And we have the voices of Leland and others essentially telling us, "Do not go there. Do not make that union. Do not give up who you are." And besides, in this union of school prayer, in this union of church and state, what church is represented? Who is the winner? Some people have come up with charts and graphs illustrating how the removal of school prayer coordinates with the decline of public schools. Yet prayer was never "removed" from schools. We need to tell our children today that they can pray in school anytime and anywhere. It is just not to be a dictated prayer delivered over the school PA system. As I point out to my students over and over again, here in the Bible Belt we think that we are going to have a nice Baptist prayer delivered. But in San Antonio, where I grew up, more often than not that prayer would be a Catholic prayer. In Utah that prayer would be a Mormon prayer. And in California all bets are off; that prayer could be most anything.

The union of church and state does not do any good for either of them. We cannot forget Baptists such as Obadiah Holmes and Samuel Harris, who were beaten and imprisoned for their Baptist beliefs. If we are willing to say that separation of church and state is a myth, and that there can be a union between the two, then we need to be willing and prepared for a government to promote a religion other than ours. And we need to be ready for the government to persecute our religion instead of someone else's. Who would support such a union? No one, I hope.

Baptists from the very beginning—Thomas Helwys, Roger Williams, George W. Truett, and many others—saw the need for that separation, saw the need to guarantee that all would be free to worship or to not worship as they chose. John Leland noted, "If the truth is great, and will prevail by itself, we wish it may be so." Why? So that the watching world will see that our faith is not based on wealth or influence. When it comes to a union of church and state, many people who look at the church think, "The only reason that you are doing this is to acquire money and power."

And Leland is telling us that we have the truth. The gospel is the truth. We should have confidence that the truth will prevail. And let the church and state remain separate, the church working to influence society and actively in government, but not seeking protection from government to benefit our belief system, because eventually the government will get to dictate that belief system. And we all know what a revolutionary church Constantine developed. We cannot let that happen.

Hebrews 12:1 portrays a great cloud of witnesses in heaven, and often, as I look back on our Baptist heritage, I think that we have that great cloud of witnesses today. We have Leland, Williams, Backus,

Truett, and others looking down upon us saying, "Let the people know that Baptists have stood for religious freedom and for separation of church and state, not because it was good for them, but because it was right."

I recently made an editorial change to the Wikipedia entry on Baptists and the separation of church and state. Unless another change has since been made, you will notice that the first line under "History" reads, "Originally Baptists supported separation of church and state, and authentic Baptists still do."[1]

Note

1. See http://en.wikipedia.org/wiki/Baptists_in_the_history_of_separation_ of_church_and_state (accessed March 22, 2011).

About the Contributors

David W. Bebbington (PhD, University of Cambridge) is professor of history at the University of Stirling, Scotland, and a Fellow of the Royal Historical Society.

Brian C. Brewer (PhD, Drew University) is assistant professor of Christian theology at the George W. Truett Theological Seminary, Baylor University.

Ronald L. Cook (PhD, Southern Baptist Theological Seminary) is associate professor of Christian scriptures and director of the Doctor of Ministry program at the George W. Truett Theological Seminary, Baylor University.

David E. Garland (PhD, Southern Baptist Theological Seminary) is dean and the William M. Hinson Professor of Christian Scriptures at the George W. Truett Theological Seminary, Baylor University.

Joel C. Gregory (PhD, Baylor University) is professor of preaching at the George W. Truett Seminary, Baylor University, and Distinguished Fellow of Georgetown College in Georgetown, Kentucky.

Carol Crawford Holcomb (PhD, Baylor University) is professor in the College of Christian Studies (Church History and Baptist Studies) at the University of Mary Hardin-Baylor in Belton, Texas.

Amy E. Jacober (PhD, Fuller Theological Seminary) is associate professor of practical theology and youth ministry at the George W. Truett Theological Seminary, Baylor University.

Alan J. Lefever (PhD, Southwestern Baptist Theological Seminary) is director of the Texas Baptist Historical Collection and adjunct professor of church history at the George W. Truett Theological Seminary, Baylor University.

Lai Ling Elizabeth Ngan (PhD, Golden Gate Baptist Theological Seminary) is associate professor of Christian scriptures at the George W. Truett Theological Seminary, Baylor University.

Roger E. Olson (PhD, Rice University) is professor of theology at the George W. Truett Theological Seminary, Baylor University.

Todd D. Still (PhD, The University of Glasgow, Scotland) is professor of Christian scriptures at the George W. Truett Theological Seminary, Baylor University.

W. Dennis Tucker Jr. (PhD, Southern Baptist Theological Seminary) is associate dean and associate professor of Christian scriptures at the George W. Truett Theological Seminary, Baylor University.

C. Douglas Weaver (PhD, Southern Baptist Theological Seminary) is associate professor of religion and coordinator of Baptist Studies for Research in the department of religion at Baylor University.

Ralph Douglas West (DMin, Beeson Divinity School, Samford University) is pastor and founder of Brookhollow Baptist Church, Houston, Texas, and adjunct professor of preaching at the George W. Truett Theological Seminary, Baylor University.

David E. Wilhite (PhD, The University of St. Andrews, Scotland) is assistant professor of Christian theology at the George W. Truett Theological Seminary, Baylor University.